Foreword

By ROB LLOYD

Two years ago I was 50, and had taught for nearly 30 years. Time for a change.

I decided to find out what higher education was like at the grass roots level. I could then return to my school better able to advise sixth-formers choosing from the tangled web of courses and institutions. My tour covered England, Wales and Scotland and included 30 colleges of higher education, all the polytechnics, and all universities except Oxford and Cambridge. In the course of these visits I led the focus group discussions for this report and then went on to ask my own set of 20 questions to thousands of additional students.

For me, six aspects stood out.

1. Students in colleges, polytechnics and universities often judge their widely different resources as being the same. For example, they may rate their library holding 20,000 books as highly as students in another institution where the library has 800,000. In a similar way they cannot appreciate where standards have fallen over the past ten years because they are in the system for such a short period of time. This lack of comparative experience tends to make them excessively tolerant and loyal to their chosen institution.

2. With striking exceptions, students are not getting enough close academic encounters in regular small group tutorials. This is partly the result of worsening staff-student ratios, but may also be affected by the other pressures now placed on teaching staff such as income generation and research.

3. Commonly, students cannot easily get the books that they are recommended to consult. The bookshops associated with the institutions are often limited so they are not exposed to a wide enough range of alternative sources even if they could afford to buy. The libraries themselves are often crowded and noisy.

4. The students' own poverty can make their lives very stressful. Accommodation and related costs are the major outlay and often consume most of the grant. It is absurd that students should be given a grant that, with the exception of London, makes no allowance for the wide range in the price of rents throughout the country. Where

iii

they were being asked for £55 per week they could not manage; on less than £20 they could scrape by.

5. Students' extra curricular activities are often very limited. This is partly due to their financial problems, but also the intensive demands of some of the more vocational courses which leave them so drained that any free time is simply used to unwind. There are often many societies which appear to be available but many fizzle out after a few weeks due to lack of support.

6. The students are increasingly feeling exploited by their institutions. They resent being packed in to bolster ailing finances. I shared a lecture room floor with several students because there were not enough seats. They often have heavy charges imposed on them and fees charged for facilities such as health centres which they might have expected to be free.

In many places the management appears to have failed to explain the overall financial position of the institution to the students and as a consequence, too few students understand the reasons behind many of the measures that are taken. Better communication between institutions and students would work wonders.

In view of these increasing problems, the need for informed choices has never been greater. Students in schools must start getting experience early by making visits to as many higher education institutions as possible during their first year of A-levels. Equally, I strongly endorse the view expressed in the conclusions of this Report that more advice is needed throughout the secondary school period. Choice of GCSEs and BTECs or A-levels needs a knowledge of the implications for higher education, and a deep assessment of the real inclinations of the individual.

Finally, I would like to express my gratitude to the many students who gave up their time to speak to me. Only four students refused to talk to me—most were very supportive, helpful and kind.

Contents

1

Chapter 1 Introduction

1.1 Purpose of the Survey

Over 5,650 students in over 100 higher education institutions took part in this survey during the period October—December 1990. The purpose and aims of the project were:

(1) to assist applicants and their advisers in schools, colleges and careers offices by articulating the experiences of previous applicants and "freshers";

(2) to help those responsible for student recruitment and public relations within higher education to understand better the needs of students, and to explain further the decision-making process that applicants use when considering higher education courses and institutions;

(3) to identify good practice in terms of customer-care and responsiveness within institutions;

(4) to discover what differences there are, if any, between the students within the three sectors of higher education and the nature of the student experience within each sector;

(5) to provide some benchmark results on a national basis which individual institutions may find useful when comparing with results from their own in-house student surveys; and

(6) to let students have their say.

When formulating higher education policy and practice, far too little effort has been made to canvass the ideas and opinions of the consumers of the service compared with the interests of academics, industry and government agencies. We hope that this report will help to redress the balance.

1.2 Methodology

(a) The Sampling Frame

The students who took part in the survey were all starting the second year of their course: they were all admitted on to that course in 1989.

Second year students were chosen because they had experienced one year of higher education and were therefore in a position to pass judgement on their institution and their course: they were also able to comment on

3

the transition into higher education and the services provided in schools and FE colleges.

To ensure that the findings of the survey were representative of higher education as a whole, the widest possible participation was sought. Institutions invited to participate were universities, polytechnics and colleges of higher education who are members of either UCCA or PCAS and/or are funded primarily through the UFC or the PCFC. Further education colleges and other specialist institutions primarily involved in further education, but who nevertheless offer some degrees or HNDs, were not included.

Undergraduate institutions which are part of the collegiate Universities of London and Wales were invited to participate as freestanding organisations.

Only institutions in England and Wales were involved in the questionnaire and focus group elements. The reason for not involving Scottish or Irish institutions is that their education systems are different from those in England and Wales in many important respects. The questions used as the basis for this research would not have been valid in many cases. However, many Scottish institutions were visited and students engaged in the semi-structured discussions.

(b) The Techniques Employed

The fieldwork for this project took place largely during the months of October, November and December 1990. The survey used three techniques to generate data:

(1) Questionnaires

Approximately 7,000 questionnaires were issued to students for completion and return. 2,818 were received representing a response rate of 40%. No financial or other incentives were offered.

The questionnaires were constructed after discussions with a number of information officers and public relations managers in higher education institutions, and other education professionals such as student counsellors.

4

The draft questionnaire was then piloted with students from Leeds Polytechnic. This helped to ensure that the questions were understandable and in the correct sequence. A number of open-ended questions were asked and in some cases the results were used to generate multiple choice questions which were still valid but required less time to complete and to compute. A number of open-ended questions remained where we felt that a multiple choice would be too leading and restrictive.

The pilot tests showed that the questionnaire took an average of 20 minutes to complete. Based on the pilot, a 35% response rate had been predicted.

All higher education institutions were asked to participate in this element of the research. Only one, a university, refused point-blank to participate. A number of others asked not to be included for technical reasons or due to pressure on staff time. In total 96 institutions agreed to take part and returns were duly received from them all.

Each institution was asked randomly to select 65 home students who were just starting the second year of a full-time advanced course (HND, DipHE or Degree). This process proved to be very difficult for some institutions which did not have computerised records.

The questionnaires were distributed to the 65 students using the institutions' internal postal systems. The students received a sealed envelope containing the questionnaire (with instructions) and a reply envelope addressed to Heist's internal contact—usually a member of the institution's registry. To ensure confidentiality the questionnaires were returned in a sealed envelope using the internal postal system. Students were given two weeks to respond, after which the envelopes, still sealed, were forwarded to Heist for validation and analysis.

Appendix 1 is a copy of the questionnaire. **Appendix 2** lists the institutions which took part in the questionnaire survey.

(2)   Focus Group Interviews

Because this project was concerned with student opinion it would have been unwise to have relied solely on the results of a postal questionnaire. The focus group interview method enabled us to ask additional questions that were deemed unsuitable for the questionnaire method. The focus groups also allowed us to go into some topics covered in the questionnaire in more depth and to help us to understand the reasoning behind some of the views that the students held: questionnaires help us to understand what students think; the focus groups help us to explore why.

This part of the research was piloted at Goldsmiths' College, University of London. The tests enabled us to make judgements about: the optimum number of students for a group (6—8), the time required to discuss the topics (60 minutes), how long the group could sustain the discussion (45—60 minutes), the practicality of using recording equipment, and the interviewer/facilitator suitability.

For the sake of consistency, only one interviewer was employed to facilitate at all of the sessions. All of the groups were tape recorded and the material transcribed onto floppy disk. This was considered to be by far the most accurate method of collecting the data. Note-taking is susceptible to interviewer fatigue and many other negative factors. The interviews generated over 90,000 words of student comment.

The interviews were organised so that they would be representative of the total population of second-year higher education students. Of the 30 institutions who were asked to participate only one declined. One university, one polytechnic and one college of higher education were selected within each of the nine regions of England and one of each type participated from Wales. As there were no polytechnics in East Anglia at the time, Anglia Higher Education College was used as a proxy polytechnic. The ten universities were also selected to reflect the different types of institution: "traditional", "red-brick", "technological", etc. The colleges were also a mixture of rural and urban institutions, and reflected the various traditions within the college sector. **Appendix 3** lists the institutions who hosted the focus group sessions.

The students were, as far as practicable, a cross section of each institution's student body—reflecting gender and subject balance. This was not always accurate because the students were volunteers and their availability depended on the timing of the focus group in relation to their study commitments.

The focus groups were structured sessions: all the groups were asked the same questions and in the same order. Supplementary questions were used where appropriate, in order to stimulate debate. The discussions took place during the period October—December 1990. A list of the questions asked is contained in **Appendix 4**.

(3)   Coffee Bar Discussions

In addition to those institutions hosting focus groups, our researcher visited most of the remaining higher education institutions in England, Wales and Scotland in his capacity as a careers/higher education teacher. These visits included informal, semi-structured "chats" with students in cafeterias, common rooms, coffee bars and students' unions. Whilst not a formal part of the research, the views of these students (2,600) have been used to validate the comments of the focus groups and the quantitative data obtained through the questionnaires. These visits took place between October 1990 and March 1991.

1.3   Statistical Presentation

In all cases the figures presented as percentages in the tables of this Report have been rounded up or down to the nearest whole figure. This is intended to facilitate easy reading of a document containing a large quantity of statistical information. However, the convention of rounding up or down does create apparent anomalies in the data which need explanation. In row one (Engineering and Technology) of **Table 5** for example, the sum of the columns for polytechnics, colleges and universities (i.e. 12% of 680, 12% of 1,084 and 8% of 1,054) does not equal 11% of all responses (i.e. 11% of 2,818). The explanation in this example, as throughout the book, is rounding. In this particular example, the total was 296 which represented 10.51 rounded up to 11.

1.4   Miscellaneous Comments

(1)   The survey was designed to focus on the traditional applicant to higher education: home-based students aged 20 and under.

7

We did however "catch" several hundred mature students in the questionnaire survey due to the random nature of the selection. Many institutions could not identify and isolate information relating specifically to mature students from their overall records. This illustrates an unexpected and remarkable paucity of management information systems. The information collected from mature students has been analysed and a separate chapter on the findings is included in this Report.

(2) A significant part of the survey required students to recall events and actions from some years previous. The pilot research discovered that students had very little difficulty in recalling the decisions that they had made at the age of 15/16+ (i.e three years earlier).

(3) The questionnaire was completed carefully in almost all cases. There were very few cases of the respondents not understanding a question or the method of response.

(4) The presence of a tape recorder did not appear to inhibit the participants in the focus groups. The students were very frank and "natural" even to the point of disclosing information of a very personal nature.

Many students were delighted that someone was asking for their opinions and listening to their concerns. Anonymity and confidentiality certainly played an important part here. It is unlikely that interviews carried out by staff from the institutions concerned would have generated such a candid set of responses.

(5) We found that university students generated 30% more material from the focus groups than polytechnic students. University students were far less likely to agree to a fellow participant's comments without adding their own input into the debate. University students seemed more able to articulate their opinions and certainly had a greater number of comments to make.

We can but only speculate as to the reasons for this. University students are probably more likely to participate in tutorial and discussion groups and may therefore be more at ease in a group situation. Perhaps their more middle class backgrounds and their previous scholastic success have created a more confident and opinionated student.

(6)   We learned a great deal about individual institutions but do not intend this book to do any more than to illustrate national trends.

Chapter 2   A Profile of the Respondents

2.1 Introduction

The questionnaire results, which form the backbone of this report, are based on a sample of 2,818 completed forms—representing a response rate of 40%. The first section of the questionnaire asked a number of general questions, from which we can build up a profile of the sample. Using this information we can measure how accurately the sample reflects the total population of students admitted in 1989. The results also provide a valuable basis for analysing the nature of the students within each of the three sectors of higher education (polytechnics, universities and colleges of higher education) and for helping to indicate the ways in which the students attending the three institutional types differ.

2.2 Institutional Type

Table 1 shows that polytechnic students form a smaller proportion (25%) of the total sample of this survey than do university or college students. This is purely a result of there being fewer polytechnic institutions: the response rate from polytechnics was relatively high at 46%. When compared with actual admissions for 1989 (43% to universities, 33% to polytechnics and 24% to colleges) the sample is biased towards the colleges of higher education at the expense of the other two sectors.

Table 1   Questionnaire responses by institutional type

	Responses	% of Sample
Polytechnic	680	25
University	1,084	38
College	1,054	37
Total	2,818	100

2.3 Gender of Respondents

Table 2 shows the gender balance of the sample. Compared with the figures for actual admissions for 1989, the sample slightly favours females. This was almost entirely due to the college responses: the polytechnic and university returns were almost 50:50 in terms of gender,

11

whereas 62% of the college respondents were female. The survey results therefore offer a slightly more feminine view of higher education than would a perfectly constructed sample.

Table 2   Analysis of the sample by gender

	M%	F%
Polytechnics	49	51
Universities	51	49
Colleges	38	62
Total	45	55

2.4   Age at Entry into Higher Education

Table 3 gives a profile of the respondents' age at entry to their current course. 85% of respondents were "traditional" admissions by age—i.e. aged 20 or under, the intended "target" of the questionnaire. There were more mature students (19%) represented in the polytechnic returns than in the other two institutional types. This would appear to reflect the wider access policies of the polytechnics and the relative attractiveness of the sector to this group.

Table 3   Age at entry into higher education

	All%	P%	U%	C%
17 and under	2	0	2	1
18	46	41	53	41
19	27	29	26	26
20	9	11	7	11
21 and over	15	19	12	21

2.5   Scholastic Origins

Table 4 gives the spread of responses by scholastic origin at the time of applying to higher education. 26% of the sample were not in one of the five main school-types at the time of applying: these were largely the mature students (15% of the sample) and those who had taken a year out after leaving school.

The sample under-represents the comprehensive school, particularly within the polytechnic sector.

Table 4   Scholastic origins of students at time of applying

	All%	P%	U%	C%
Comprehensive	24	21	27	23
FE college	17	24	8	23
Independent school	11	6	19	7
Grammar school	8	7	10	5
Sixth-form college	13	14	14	12
Other (FT education)	6	7	6	5
Full time employment	13	14	11	15
None of above	7	7	5	10
No response	1	7	0	0

The figures in **Table 4** highlight some of the differences between polytechnic and university students: polytechnic students are more likely to come from a further education college than their university counterparts by a factor of 3 (8% against 24%). The positions are reversed when examining independent schools (a factor of 3.16 in favour of the universities). Despite the fact that many colleges offer university-validated degrees and heavily promote their associations with the university sector, the figures suggest that the colleges are no more attractive to the grammar and independent sectors than are polytechnics.

Sixth-form colleges appear to be evenly represented in all sectors. Previous Heist/PCAS research (1) has shown that pupils from these schools were the most knowledgeable about higher education and the options open to them. Being concerned mainly with 16-19 year-olds who are likely to continue their education, advice about higher education will naturally form a more important part of the curriculum in such colleges. The more even spread of sixth-form college students throughout the three sectors perhaps indicates that their choices are less based on prejudice and more related to decisions about what is the right course/institutional mix for them as individuals.

2.6 Subject Area

Table 5 gives the breakdown of the sample by subject of study. Most students had little difficulty in categorising their courses—the only problems were encountered by those pursuing joint honours or modular programmes. The subject categories are largely based on Universities Funding Council and Polytechnics and Colleges Funding Council definitions.

The sample is short of respondents in Built Environment (Architecture, Building, Planning, etc.), IT/Computing, and Medicine. Medical students are often off-campus and perhaps too occupied to complete questionnaires. Perhaps Humanities and Business students are more willing and likely to complete questionnaires because of the nature of their studies?

The figures help to illustrate the subject strengths of the three sectors. The colleges are very strongly represented in Teacher Training, Creative Arts and Humanities, the universities in the Sciences and Humanities (particularly English, History, Languages and Geography), whilst the polytechnics appear as more diverse institutions, majoring in Business.

Table 5   Subject area of study

	All%	**P%**	**U%**	**C%**
Engineering and Technology	11	12	12	8
Built Environment	3	6	1	2
Science and Maths	12	12	22	3
IT and Computing	5	8	3	3
Business (including Law)	19	26	15	18
Health and Social Services	2	3	1	1
Humanities and Social Sciences	25	16	38	22
Art/Design/Music/Drama	12	11	3	20
Education/Teacher Training	10	5	1	23
Medicine/Dentistry	1	1	1	0

2.7   Catchment Areas

The survey asked the students to estimate the approximate distance between their place of study and their parental home. We must treat the figures in **Table 6** with some caution, but they do give us a general pattern.

A sizeable number of students still study at a local institution. 14% of respondents' parental homes were within an estimated 19 miles of their place of study and a total of 23% were within 39 miles. Many commentators have suggested that the introduction of student loans and the freezing of the maintenance grant will encourage more students to "live at home and study locally". Further research in a few years' time, when student loans have taken hold, would throw light on this contention.

The disaggregated figures are very interesting. They reveal that university students are far more likely to study well away from home than their polytechnic or college counterparts. A striking 64% are studying at least 100 miles from their parental home, compared with only 43% of college students and 50% of polytechnic students. Polytechnics were originally created to have a more regional focus and they certainly appear to attract greater numbers of "local students" than do the universities. However, in terms of local recruitment, the colleges leave the rest standing. A remarkable 34% of college students are studying at a college within daily travelling distance of home (39 miles). These figures perhaps reflect the more mature nature of the college/polytechnic student body.

As we reveal later (**Table 22**), the strategic location of an institution and, in particular, its distance from the applicant's home, is a very important criterion for students when making their choice of institution. 29% of the respondents placed this in their "top three" criteria and 11% said that it was the most important factor, thereby putting it on a par with "reputation, recommendation and status".

We hypothesised that most school-leavers preferred to leave their home area to gain a level of independence but try to remain within reasonable travelling distance of home to facilitate those essential "laundry" visits. The median distance for all students fell into the range of 100—119 miles, which is less than three hours by most forms of transport, but too far for the so-called "unwanted" parental visits.

Individual institutions will have different catchment profiles, depending on the demography of their home region and their strategic location within the country. Centrally-located institutions with good access will invariably attract more students from outside their region than institutions in more peripheral coastal areas.

Table 6   Distance from parental home

Miles	All%	P%	U%	C%
00-19	14	16	6	21
20-39	9	7	6	13
40-59	8	9	8	7
60-79	8	9	9	7
80-99	6	7	6	6
100-119	8	7	10	7
120-139	8	8	8	7
140-159	6	6	7	4
160+	31	29	39	25
No response	2	2	1	3

2.8 Type of Course Studied

Respondents were asked to identify the type of course on which they were studying. 80% were on the traditional honours degree programmes, with 12% on BTEC HNDs.

The honours degree remains dominant in the universities, but less so in the college/polytechnic sectors, where large numbers are studying for HNDs. The DipHE has become rather unfashionable in recent years and is generally offered as a terminal qualification only to those who have successfully completed at least two years of a degree programme but who decide not to continue their studies. It will be interesting to plot the increasing attractiveness of the DipHE as it is now being awarded to those studying for two-year qualifications in Social Work and Nursing. We are beginning to wonder whether two-year higher education qualifications might not one day become the norm.

Table 7 Type of course

	All%	P%	U%	C%
Honours degree	80	79	93	71
Degree	5	4	5	6
DipHE	1	1	0	2
HND	12	15	1	20
Other	1	1	1	1

2.9 Urban/Rural Origins

Students were asked to indicate in what sort of locality they had been residing at the time of making their application to higher education. The intention was to test for any correlation between the nature of the home environment and choice of institutional location (i.e. is a student from a city more likely to go to an urban-based institution and do rural students prefer an out-of-town campus or rural-based college?).

The overall results for this question were intriguing. The majority of the UK population is classified as being urban (77% lived in towns and cities with a population of 50,000 or more according to the 1981 census) yet these areas only account for 43% of the respondents to our survey. If the student population as a whole mirrors our sample it begs a number of questions.

Is the nature of teaching in rural areas more geared towards higher education?

Are urban school pupils in some way disadvantaged when it comes gaining entry to higher education?

Do the results reflect the class bias of higher education: rural areas being more middle class than urban areas?

Polytechnics appear to attract a slightly larger proportion of students from urban areas (47%) than either the universities (44%) or the colleges (40%). These figures perhaps indicate that the location of the institution does have some effect: the majority of polytechnics are based in major cities or in other urban settings, whereas the colleges tend to be located in towns and rural settings. Universities fall somewhere between the two: some city-based, some on suburban campuses.

Various studies have shown (2) that the specific location of an institution is important to applicants and 37% of respondents in this survey placed it as the most important factor influencing their choice, with 52% placing it amongst their top three. However, only 4% said that the rural/campus/city factor had been an influence. Perhaps this urban/rural factor is subconscious.

An alternative explanation for the relative attractiveness of polytechnics to urban applicants is the nature of the courses and the subjects offered by them. Applicants from industrial and commercial centres are more likely to be exposed to the world of work and may be influenced to pursue a more vocational form of higher education.

Table 8 Urban/rural origins

	All%	P%	U%	C%
Rural area	26	25	26	26
Small town	31	28	31	34
Major town	20	25	18	20
City	23	22	25	19

More detailed analysis of the data does suggest that there is a weak positive correlation between the nature of the home address of the applicant and that of the institution at which they are studying. The urban universities in the survey had higher proportions of urban students (49%) than those in campus/rural locations (41%). It was difficult to repeat this analysis for the polytechnics as most were urban-based and many students in the sector were not at their first-choice institution. Any analysis that could be done did support the university results, although less positively.

2.10 Entry Qualifications

Based on the system whereby an A grade at A-level constitutes 10 points, the students were asked "how many A-level points did you achieve before entering higher education?" A-level grades are (regrettably) still the main measure used by admissions tutors for determining entry to advanced courses—despite the lack of evidence to show that they are a good predictor of degree performance.

Although the vast majority had taken at least one A-level or AS level, many other qualifications were gained of an equivalent nature such as BTEC National Diplomas: these were noted but were not given a numerical weighting.

The average points level attained by our sample of students was 14.1 which roughly equates to the following combinations: BC; AD; CDD; BDE. The modal figure was 11 points and the median score was 14.

**Table 8   Average A-level points by subject (degree only—
        all institutions)**

Science/Maths	19.1
Humanities/Social Science	17.6
Engineering/Technology	16.4
Business/Law	16.0
Health/Social Services	15.2
Built Environment	14.4
Art/Design/Music/Drama	14.3
Education/Teacher Training	13.5
IT/Computing	11.3

Table 8 shows the breakdown of points by the subject of study. It is interesting that two of the subject areas that were keen to attract applications in 1989—Sciences and Engineering—attracted students with relatively high points scores. Student recruiters in shortage areas have claimed that high entry requirements (the price of gaining entry to a course) will deter applicants, and have suggested that courses that find it difficult to fill all their places may be "pricing" themselves out of the

market. It is received wisdom that courses which find it difficult to recruit, notably in Mathematics, Engineering and the pure Sciences, reduce their entry requirements. Our findings might suggest that this is not the case but our survey deals with students who have reached their second year. Perhaps many of those admitted with lower grades dropped out, for whatever reason, in their first-year. Research into this aspect of student "wastage" would be invaluable. Those courses with a surplus of applicants, such as Business and Law, have been able to increase entry requirements as a means of raising status and managing demand.

Chapter 3   Choices in Schools

3.1   Introduction

How and why students make their choices at 16+ are of great importance both to careers advisers and those trying to recruit into higher
education. In this chapter we cover the choices at 16+, the age at which
decisions relating to higher education are made, who advises and who
influences applicants/students, and what criteria applicants use when
short-listing institutions.

3.2   Subject Choices at 16+

The focus group interview groups spent some considerable time dis-
cussing A-level and BTEC subject choices and how they were made. The
following conclusions were drawn:

(1) Most chose subjects that they had "enjoyed" or were successful at in GCSEs: normally these were one and the same.
When choosing three subjects most said that two were easy to
choose but that the third option took a little thought.

(2) The majority chose to follow only "Arts" or only "Science"
combinations. Three reasons emerged:

(a) In some cases the school timetable would not allow
combinations across the Arts-Science line. This problem
appears to be declining.

(b) Most claimed that taking three Arts or three Science
subjects was the "natural thing to do"—their three
favourite subjects tended to cluster.

(c) Many said that choosing three Arts/Science subjects was
sensible because they inter-related well in terms of study
skills and methods of learning. They also attracted like-
minded people which led to a better social atmosphere.

Many who had taken three science or technical subjects at A-
level said that in retrospect they wished that they had not
specialised to such an extent. Interestingly no interviewee who
had taken all Arts/Humanities subjects at school said that he
or she regretted that decision.

(3) When choosing the third (or fourth) subject many students had been influenced most by their parents who wanted them to choose a "good or useful subject". Economics was the subject most often cited as being "useful". 5% of the interviewees said that HE entry requirements had influenced their choice of the third A-level—almost all were science-based students who felt that many HE institutions required three science subjects for a lot of Science/Engineering courses.

(4) Some chose a "new subject" to study at 16+. Classical Civilisation was mentioned by a number of interviewees—all of whom thought it had been enjoyable and useful.

(5) Many sixth-form teachers appear actively to recruit students for their subjects. Sixth-formers were certainly attracted to subjects taught by "good teachers" based on their GCSE experiences. Better teachers were seen as providing a greater chance of good grades.

(6) The students had a number of complaints to make about choices at 16+:

(i) The level of advice from schools at 16+ regarding subject choice was very poor when compared with advice about higher education given in the sixth-form. Many felt that options had been closed to them because they took the wrong A-level combinations at 16+.

(ii) There was too much pressure from schools to do Sciences and AS levels—neither of which were seen as attractive to those who had not taken these routes.

(iii) Schools encouraged many to opt for a "balancing subject" as the third choice. Many of those who had failed at least one A-level claimed that it was this subject that they failed—a subject that they would not have normally considered. Many felt that a place on a good HE course had been lost because they had acted upon poor advice rather than following their natural interests at 16+.

(iv) There was little enthusiasm for the introduction of broader qualifications at 16+ because the students felt that it would have forced them to study subjects in which they had little interest or ability: they feared poorer grades as a consequence. Good grades, and the sense of achievement that went with them, were very important to the students.

Student Comments

I chose English and History because they were the subjects that I enjoyed most. I opted for Classical Civilisation which is the most useful A-level that I've done. Invaluable ever since.

I went for my best grades and the ones I enjoyed.

I chose Physics and Chemistry because I couldn't write very well.

I went for the ones I was good at and those I enjoyed—the same.

I chose English, History and French. I find that in the Arts you can express yourself, which I like.

I chose Maths, Physics and Chemistry—they went together very well.

I thought about doing Engineering. It was fairly obvious—Maths Physics and Chemistry.

My school was constrained towards Sciences. I did Maths Physics and Chemistry because that was all that was really open to me. I would have liked to have done History or English but it didn't work out on the timetable.

Everyone advised me to do Maths, Physics and Chemistry for Engineering but I knew I would fail Chemistry so I did Geography instead. It turned out to be a good move as Civil Engineering has more Geography than Chemistry.

I chose Maths, Physics and Chemistry as these were the ones that the teachers pushed for people who didn't know what to do.

Originally I wanted to do French, Geography and Biology. The tutor said I should do all Sciences. I ended up doing quite badly and then I re-sat them and did badly again.

People told me that Sciences were the things to do—foolishly I went along with them. I am now into a less scientific subject Psychology.

I did Chemistry, Physics and Biology. I would rather have done Geography.

I decided to do Sociology, History and Biology, but Biology didn't work out at all with Sociology and History so I dropped it and did Politics in a year.

I chose English and British Politics because I thought it would be useful. It wasn't.

I did BTEC Business Studies. It sounded different and more interesting than O-levels.

I did History, Sociology and Politics. I chose Sociology because I thought it was a soft option. I was wrong.

If we didn't get a "B" at O-level you couldn't do it at A-level.

I changed school because they wanted me to do Latin. No way!

I didn't get any advice from my school at all (a comment made by many respondents).

I started A-levels but hated them. I switched to BTECs.

3.3 Employment vs Higher Education

The students were asked if they had seriously considered some form of employment as an alternative to higher education (serious consideration being defined as applying for a job or at least writing for job details). As **Table 9** shows, 27% had seriously considered the alternative of employment. Far fewer university students had considered the employment alternative than had their counterparts in polytechnics.

Table 9 Whilst in the sixth-form, did you seriously consider employment as an alternative to higher education?

	All%	P%	U%	C%
Yes	27	30	20	24
No	66	61	76	58
Can't remember	2	3	2	3
No response	5	6	2	15

3.4 Motivation for Higher Education

So what is the great attraction of further study? What motivates young people to continue in, or return to, education, rather than directly enter the job market after school and pursue a career? The focus groups considered both of these questions.

The top six reasons (in descending order) given to the three linked questions "Why did you stay on in higher education?" "What do you students get out of it?" "What makes it worthwhile?" were:

(1) **The natural thing to do (peer and parental pressure).**

For many students (particularly those in universities) one of the biggest decisions of their life was in reality a non-decision.

I was brought-up with the idea of going to university. (U)

There is no-one in our family who hasn't got a degree. (U)

Neither of my parents have been through higher education and they said you are going—FULL STOP. (P)

I never considered not going into college! (C)

(2) **Improves job prospects in the long-term**

This was cited more often by polytechnic students than by those at college or university.

People want graduates and you start one or two steps up the ladder. (P)

I was a chef. I never had much job satisfaction—I wasn't going to be a another Roux brother. (P)

I didn't want to get halfway up the management ladder and find people with degrees getting the top jobs. I wanted an exciting job at the top. (C)

I saw that a degree was necessary in the careers world today—especially in getting jobs away from the area I was brought up in. (U)

You get control of your life. (U)

(3) Postpones the need to work

This was cited more often by university students than those in colleges or polytechnics.

If you go into a job at 18 you will work for 40 years. I want to put off working for as long as possible. (U)

I had four weeks experience in a travel agent and hated it—I wasn't mature enough at 18. (P)

I was too lazy to get a job. (C)

You can surround yourself with like-minded people and no factory whistle to make them disappear. (U)

(4) Postpones the need to make a career decision—time to think

Initially I came because I didn't know what I wanted to do career-wise and I thought that I might as well keep learning until I did decide. (P)

I think that many students of 18 don't know what they want to do—it's a way of bridging the gap and giving them a few more years spent constructively before they have to decide what they want to do. (P)

(5) Allows students to pursue knowledge/interest in chosen subject

Almost exclusively cited by university students.

I love studying and writing essays. (U)

A test of what I could achieve. (U)

I was interested in Maths and wanted to find out more. I am disillusioned—you expect to find people in groups talking about intellectual things but it's not like that.(U)

(6) Allows students to become independent

A stepping-stone to reality. (U)

You get an overall development, you get an academic development and you develop socially. Your whole self changes. (P)

You are experiencing more things from different angles that you wouldn't experience if you went straight out to work. (P)

You notice how much you have changed when you go back home. The friends are still the same but I am glad that I'm changing. You appreciate your parents more. (P)

It is a gentle introduction to being an adult and growing up! (P)

I lived a sheltered life in Cornwall—this was my big chance to go. (U)

Having been closeted in a girls' school for years, it is quite educational to be let out amongst men! (U)

The questionnaire survey asked students at what age they had firmly decided to aim for higher education. The majority (64%) said that their minds were made up before entering the sixth-form or further education. Given this result, and bearing in mind students' views that they were given poor advice at 16+, schools should surely be looking to give at least some initial advice and guidance about higher education well before the third term of the lower sixth the usual time for higher education advice to begin. More informed choices at 16+ or before would lead to better decisions at 18.

The figures again show that the universities are attracting a different sort of student—those for whom higher education seems to have been a natural choice from a very early age. As shown later in this Report, university students are much more likely to have at least one parent who has a degree. In such circumstances higher education becomes the norm rather than the exception.

Table 10   Age at which firmly decided to aim for higher education

	All%	P%	U%	C%
Before 16	64	54	72	58
16-18	19	22	15	22
19 and after	17	24	13	20
Average	15.2	15.7	14.7	15.8
Mode	16	16	16	16

3.5 Age at Which Choice of Higher Education Subject was Made

The results to the question "At what age did you firmly decide on your choice of higher education subject?" are contained in **Table 11**. The greatest proportion of students decided on their higher education subject in the sixth-form years (46%). Once again, university students seem to make their choices slightly earlier.

Those professions and subject-interest groups which are currently spending a great deal of resources to try and persuade young people to choose courses in their field should note that a large proportion (29%) had already decided upon their subject before entering the sixth-form phase of their education. No doubt many of those who finally made a firm decision in the sixth-form will have been formulating their ideas for some little time.

Table 11(a) gives the data on age by subject area. The results are reasonably consistent with two notable exceptions. A very high proportion (70%) of Science and Mathematics students decided on the subject during the sixth-form years. This suggests that A-level or BTEC Science gripped the imagination of young people in a way in which O-levels had not done. Sciences do not appear to be "natural choices"— only 5% had decided upon this route by the age of 16. Something or somebody obviously converts many students during the sixth-form years. Conversely, students following studies in Art/Drama/Music and Design are much more likely to have decided upon these subjects before 16 (46%).

Table 11 Age at which firm choice of higher education subject was made

	All%	P%	U%	C%
Before 16	29	28	29	28
16-18	46	44	50	43
19 and after	25	28	21	29
Average	17.2	17.3	17.1	17.2
Mode	17	17	17	18

Table 11(a) Age at which firm choice of higher education subject was made by subject area

	Before 16	16-18	19 +
All	29	46	25
Engineering/Technology	25	48	27
Built Environment	22	50	28
Science/Maths	5	70	25
Computing/IT	23	52	25
Business/Law	25	52	23
Health/Social Services	21	47	32
Humanities/Social Science	21	47	32
Art/Design/Music/Drama	46	32	21
Teacher Training	26	47	24

3.6 Higher Education Advisers

The survey has attempted to identify those who advise higher education applicants about their choices, who actually influences their decision-making (a subtle difference) and what is the nature of the advice/influence.

Table 12 shows that 80% of the students took advice from either a teacher or a careers adviser before applying to higher education. Almost half (45%) spoke to more than one adviser. The widespread use of such a range of advisers was something of a surprise. The form teacher and specific subject teachers clearly have a significant role. This creates a problem for those who are specifically responsible for disseminating information about higher education and who aim positively to influence advisers. Simply mailing the careers teacher is clearly not the answer. Gaining access to these other "advisers" within schools is not easily achieved, however.

The LEA careers adviser is clearly the leading player when it comes to college and polytechnic students: in most cases they are the main source of information for non-traditional students who do not have access to counsellors within schools.

20% of the sample took no advice at all before applying. This is a very disturbing figure. Whether this lack of advice affected the quality of the decisions that the students made is difficult to assess.

Table 12   Discussed higher education plans before applying with...

	All%	P%	U%	C%
Careers adviser (LEA)	44	46	36	44
Careers teacher	37	40	47	37
Head/principal	13	12	17	13
Form/house master	22	25	35	22
Subject teacher	29	23	35	29
None of above	20	21	16	20

What was the nature of the advice that was given by the counsellors listed in **Table 12**? Most careers advisers would claim that it is not their job to advise students about the merits of specific courses and colleges. Indeed, with well over 150 higher education institutions, and thousands of courses, such a task is impossible. That 22% **(Table 13)** claim that their adviser recommended a specific institution is surprising: one must question the basis on which this advice was given, for it may well be out-of-date or based on anecdotal information. In some cases courses are unique or the applicant, for personal reasons, may wish to apply to a local college. In these circumstances such direct advice may be warranted. This may explain why 26% of college students were advised in this way.

Table 13   If you took advice, did your careers adviser(s) recommend a specific institution to you?

	All%	P%	U%	C%
Yes	22	19	19	26
No	78	81	81	74

Table 14 highlights that whilst advisers are, in general, unwilling to recommend specific institutions, they are much more likely (51%) to recommend a specific type of institution. This fact indicates that careers advisers believe that the three sectors are different and that those differences are important to students.

Table 14   If you took advice, did your careers adviser(s) recommend a specific type of institution?

	All%	P%	U%	C%
Yes	51	41	60	47
No	49	59	40	53

Those students who had received advice about institutional types were then asked which *specific type* of institution had been recommended to them.

Table 15   If your adviser recommended a type of institution which type did he or she recommend?

	All%	P%	U%	C%
Polytechnic	31	86	34	47
University	45	51	100	38
College of HE	16	23	5	55
Specialist College	8	6	4	26

The first statistic to note in **Table 15** is that the majority of students are now studying at the type of institution which their advisers had recommended (although in a third of cases two types of institution were recommended). This appears to suggest that where this advice is given it is generally followed. It may also be an indication of the ability of the adviser to assess the chances of an applicant gaining entry to certain types of institution—those likely to get poor grades are unlikely to be advised to apply to certain universities, for example.

The left-hand column again provides evidence that careers advisers do not equate higher education solely with universities; indeed, the majority of this sample were advised to apply to other types of institution. However, if the figures are weighted to take into account the fact that the sample over-represents the college of higher education sector it shows that 50% of the students were advised to go to universities, 38% to polytechnics and 12% to colleges.

The 80% who had taken some sort of careers advice were asked to rate the quality of that advice in the light of their subsequent experiences. Overall, the results were more positive than negative: **Table 16** shows that 46% of the respondents believed that the advice had been excellent or good compared with 19% who claimed that it had been poor or bad. We must remember that all of the respondents had completed their first-year successfully. Most of the students who drop out do so in the first year and these people (over 10% of first-year intake) are not reflected in this sample. This group may have been less enthusiastic about the advice that they had received.

31

Table 16   In the light of your experiences, how do you rate the advice that you received?

	All%	P%	U%	C%
Excellent	9	10	8	9
Good	37	36	36	38
Fair	35	34	36	36
Poor	15	14	16	13
Bad	4	6	4	4

3.7   Relatives and Friends

There is plenty of anecdotal evidence to suggest that friends and relatives do influence applicants—some offer direct guidance; some put pressure on applicants to apply to certain institutions. In some cases the advice is direct; in others the influence is probably subconscious and subliminal. *Young People's Knowledge of Higher Education* (1) showed that friends and family were mentioned by 30.6% of sixth-formers as an influence in their higher education decision-making process. This figure rose to 36.2% for those in the first half of their lower-sixth—the age when the "average" applicant makes his or her choice of higher education subject (**Table 11**).

To what extent do friends and relatives influence the choice of the subject/career made by students? **Table 17** shows that 39% of the students had a close friend or relative with a degree in a subject similar to that which they were studying or knew someone engaged in a related profession. This very high figure suggests that there must be some form of influence. In such circumstances the student is likely to have had greater exposure to the subject or to the profession in question. The success of the friend or relative may have encouraged or inspired him or her to follow in their footsteps—acting as some form of role model.

Table 17 Students with a close friend or immediate relative with a degree (or similar) or who is employed, in a field related to current subject of study.

	Yes %	No %
All	39	61
Polytechnic	39	61
University	35	65
College	44	56

Of those students with a close friend or immediate relative with experience of their subject or intended career, a remarkable 82% had discussed their plans with them (**Table 18**). This represents 32% of the whole sample and is distinctly consistent with the findings of *Young People's Knowledge of Higher Education* (1). This surely has major implications for the channels of communication used by those trying to influence subject and career choices. The figures are very consistent across the three sectors, but note that more students in HE colleges discussed the issues "in-depth". This probably reflects the specialist nature of many courses in the college sector.

Table 18 Those responding "Yes" in Table 17 who had discussed their career/educational plans with friend/relative.

	Yes—in depth %	Yes—not in depth %	No %	Can't Remember %
All	35	47	16	2
Polytechnic	31	53	15	1
University	32	51	16	1
College	39	43	16	2

Marketers and student recruiters in individual institutions will be keen to know whether the friends and relatives suggested specific institutions to the students during these discussions. The answer (**Table 19**) is "yes" but only in 33% of the cases. This represents 10% of all students in the sample. Again, one must question the basis of this advice. Did they recommend the institution that they attended x years ago? We do not know the answer but if it was "yes" it would have important implications in terms of the efforts put into fostering good alumni relations.

Table 19 Students whose close friend/immediate relative suggested specific institutions

	Yes %	No %	Can't Remember %
All	33	67	<1
Polytechnics	30	69	1
Universities	32	68	0
Colleges	35	65	0

Base: Those who had spoken to such a friend/relative.

As well as giving direct advice or information, it seems likely that parents influence their offspring's educational path indirectly through the effect of their own education background (perhaps subconsciously). The hypotheses were that children of parents with a degree are more likely to enter higher education than the population as a whole and that students with "university" parents are more likely to study at universities than at other types of institution.

The first case appears to be proved (as much as anything can be in the social sciences) by the figures in **Table 20**. 39% of the students in the survey had at least one parent with a degree or similar. Most of these parents would be at least 40 years old when their offspring entered higher education in 1989. We estimate that only 5% of 40 year-olds in the country as a whole could be expected to have a degree or similar. This indicates that higher education students are more likely to have at least one parent with a degree than their age group as a whole by a factor of eight.

Closer examination of the figures shows that approximately 13% of students have two parents with a degree or similar.

Some may use these figures to argue that higher education is still for an educational elite but they also indicate that almost two thirds of students do not come from families where a degree is the norm. However, the university sector does appear to admit a much higher proportion of students who have a family history of higher education (47%). Does the question on the UCCA form about parental occupation have an influence on admissions tutors?

Table 20   Students with at least one parent with a degree (or similar)

	All%	P%	U%	C%
Yes	39	35	47	35
No	61	65	53	65

The questionnaire then asked from which type of institution the parents had gained the qualification. **Table 21** shows that 27% of students have a parent with a university degree, compared with 26% for one of the three college categories. Only 4% of students have a parent with a polytechnic degree.

There is evidence that parents have, to date, preferred their children to go to a university rather than a polytechnic. This may also be explained by our results which show that only a small minority of parents of current students have any direct experience of studying at a polytechnic compared with those with university experience (ratio approximately 7:1). In such circumstances a bias towards the universities is hardly surprising. As more and more sixth-formers are likely to have "polytechnic parents", the nature of parental influence on applicants may change dramatically through the 1990s.

If there is a link between the educational background of the parent and the type of institution at which the child studies, then the polytechnics can expect to make great strides during the 1990s as their early graduates from the 1970s begin to influence their offspring. The first polytechnics were designated a little over 20 years ago so that it is only from the mid to late 1980s that their graduates are likely, in any significant numbers, to be parents of 18 year-old applicants to higher education.

Table 21   Nature of degrees held by the parents of current students

Institution	All%	P%	U%	C%
Polytechnic	4	4	4	3
University	27	20	41	17
Art college	2	1	2	4
Teacher college	14	15	15	14
HE college	10	11	11	9
Open university	4	2	5	3
Don't know	4	3	3	4
No degree	60	65	53	65

3.8   Criteria for Short-listing Institutions

The questionnaire asked students to list the three most important criteria that they had used to short-list those institutions to which they would apply. **Table 22** gives the top ten criteria based on all mentions.

Table 22   Criteria used by students to short-list institutions to which they would apply

Top ten answers to an open question.
All mentions.

	All%	P%	U%	C%
Course content/options	63	63	68	58
Town/city/area	52	54	59	45
Reputation/recommendation	30	32	35	23
Distance from home	29	30	23	36
Entry requirements	15	16	17	13
First impressions/atmosphere	10	7	11	8
Academic support facilities	9	12	9	13
Social facilities	8	9	10	6
Housing/accommodation	6	4	8	6
Size of the institution	6	3	6	8

The content of the course, and in particular the options available, was cited by almost two thirds of students. This is particularly important in subject areas where there are many courses with similar titles such as Business Studies. It is therefore very important for prospectuses to contain good information about the content of the courses on offer and how they differ from similar programmes elsewhere.

It would appear that the reputation of the town/city in which an institution is located is of more importance to potential applicants than the reputation of the institution itself. This again has implications for the prospectus editor who needs to ensure that the book gives full information about the host town or city.

Table 6 gave details relating to "distance from home". 29% said that this was a "top three factor" when deciding where to apply, some preferring to stay very local—others to distance themselves from their parents. It is important that prospectuses should include strategic maps showing the location of the institution. Sixth-former geographical knowledge is not always as good as many prospectus editors believe.

Entry requirements were rated fifth in the list of criteria. We note that many prospectuses do not state the specific entry requirement for courses, thereby making life somewhat difficult for applicants for whom the grades required is an important factor and who therefore have to spend cash on buying *University Entrance* or *Degree Course Offers*. Alternatively it might mean that applicants are badly advised and do not apply tactically in accordance with entry criteria.

In addition to the top ten list above, other factors mentioned were: age/gender/race ratios, teaching quality, costs, sponsorship, course assessment (examination or continuous), campus or city-based, sports facilities, pass rates and teaching methods.

The figures in **Table 22** refer to all mentions. If we disaggregate the statistics and focus on the first choices only (i.e. the most important factor cited by the students), a slightly different picture emerges. Course content and options become even more important—placed as the most important criterion by 43%. Other factors tend to be much less significant with the town/city being mentioned by 14%, reputation/ recommendation (institution) by 13%, distance from home 12% and entry grades by 7%. No other factor was mentioned by more than 2% of the respondents.

When considering these "first choice factors" we noted that distance from home was much less important to university students than to those in colleges and polytechnics. However, reputation/recommendation, not surprisingly, plays a more important (but still relatively small) part in the short-listing process.

Finally in this section, we asked the students whether their present institution was the one that they had most wanted to attend. The figures in **Table 23** may of course reflect an element of "post-admission reappraisal". We did include the option "can't remember" for those with a guilty conscience!

Table 23   Is your present college the one that you most wanted to attend?

	All%	P%	U%	C%
Yes	65	56	71	65
No	32	40	27	31
Can't remember	3	4	2	4

The figures suggest that most students gain admission to their "first choice college". There are fewer polytechnic students (56%) at their first choice than university (72%) or college (65%) students. Perhaps many polytechnic students have had to "trade down" due to poorer A-level results (Table 8) having failed to get into university.

Chapter 4 The Admissions Process and Transition to Higher Education

4.1 Introduction

In this chapter we examine the admissions process and the transition from school or FE college into higher education. We examine the nature of interviews and open days, the information sent to new entrants, and the nature of the induction programme and the students' opinions of it. We also explore the students' views on how well schools or FE colleges prepare them, both academically and socially, for higher education.

4.2 Interviews and Open Days

70% of the students had attended either an open day or an interview for the course on which they were studying. There are two important statistics to note from **Table 24**. First, a very high proportion (74%) of college students had been for an interview. This probably reflects the type of courses being studied such as Teaching (where interviews are a prerequisite for entry) and creative subjects (where auditions or portfolio presentations are the norm). It may also be due to the fact that most college courses attract fewer applications than similar ones in the other two sectors thereby allowing tutors to interview a larger proportion of the applicants. Second, only 26% of polytechnic students had attended an interview. There are two partial explanations. Perhaps the polytechnics rely more on the application form and less on time-consuming interviews. This may be true in subjects such as Business where 20 applications per place are not uncommon. The second reason for the low figure may be that the course was chosen in clearing and interviews were not available. This hypothesis is perhaps supported by the figures in **Table 23**.

Table 24 **Proportion of students attending interviews or open days for present course.**

	All%	P%	U%	C%
Interview	49	26	45	64
Open day	21	26	29	10
Neither	20	36	16	16
No response	10	12	10	10

We have already shown that first impressions (which would normally be at an interview/open day) are important when applicants decide where to apply (**Table 22**). The interview/open-day is therefore an important public relations activity. The questionnaire listed eight open day/interview activities and asked the students to indicate which had been included at their event. The results are shown in **Table 25**.

Table 25   Activities included in open days/interviews

	All%	P%	U%	C%
Contact with other applicants	89	73	94	83
Tour of college/department	88	73	95	80
A talk with staff	70	63	73	63
Contact with current students	69	50	77	66
Visit to the students' union	40	29	55	27
Time to tour town/city	26	20	34	19
Video/AV presentation	20	21	27	10
Seeing "live classes"	8	8	6	9

Base: Those who had attended an interview or open day.

The most common feature of interviews and open days is, not surprisingly, contact with other applicants. The quality of this contact is difficult to determine. Most applicants also get an opportunity to tour the college or department, talk to staff and make contact with current students. Statistics contained later in this report show that most second-year students would recommend their course and college. If interviews and open days are seen by the institution as an opportunity to promote their wares, then every effort should be made to allow current students to talk to interviewees. This should also be of value to the interviewees as they will doubtless have many questions that they are unwilling or unable to ask of staff.

Earlier figures indicate the importance of the town or city in the applicants' decision-making, yet only 26% claimed that the interview or open day gave them any time to tour the area. The services offered by students' unions are also important to applicants but only 40% were given the opportunity to visit the union at the interview/open day. The students' unions are missing a great opportunity to sell themselves and their facilities to potential students. Students' union representatives should ensure that a guided tour of the union is offered as part of all open days and, where possible, to interviewees.

The questionnaire then asked the students who had attended an interview or open-day to choose (from a list of six) the adjectives that best described the atmosphere and nature of the event.

Table 26 Nature of interviews/open days

	All%	P%	U%	C%
Casual	76	76	79	72
Inspiring	31	29	32	31
Formal	20	13	21	23
Easy	16	15	18	15
Rigorous	12	8	13	13
Dull	6	6	8	4

The majority of students described the interview or open day as casual rather than formal (ratio 3.8:1); inspiring rather than dull (ratio 5.2:1) and easy rather than rigorous (ratio 1.3:1).

We must remember that in 1989—the year these students were admitted, higher education was attempting (successfully) to expand. It was a buyers' market, and admissions tutors were largely in recruitment mode rather than acting out the role of "gatekeeper".

The fact that 31% of students were inspired at their interview is very pleasing. It is also good to report that higher education interviews are described by most as "casual". The days when applicants were intimidated by dons in flowing gowns have almost disappeared: only one in five described the interview as "formal".

These results have implications for careers advisers and others in schools and FE colleges who counsel applicants about interview techniques. It is important for these advisers to discriminate between interviews with employers and those for higher education. As the students in the focus groups testified they are very different in nature. The focus groups were asked to discuss their interviews and to offer advice to potential applicants and, where relevant, admissions tutors.

The first point was that the nature of the interview depended to a large extent upon the subject area: an interview for a Law degree would be unlike one for a Fine Art course. Again, the students claimed that sixth-form advisers too often failed to appreciate this.

41

Most students had been advised to dress formally—as if the interview were for a job. Many claimed that this was bad advice: it made the interviewees stand-out in a sea of denim and they felt more nervous and self-conscious as a result. Some claimed to have worn their best suits only to have been faced with a lecturer in jeans and a tee-shirt. The students felt that it was in both sides' interests that the applicants were comfortable during the interview. They advised admissions tutors to give interviewees an indication of the standard of dress required when making the interview invitation. If this advice wasn't forthcoming the students urged applicants to telephone the department and ask. Given the casual nature of most higher education interviews, the students felt that the importance attached to dress and appearance by teachers and parents was too great. PCAS has recently published a training package on interview technique (3) which has sold very well. Teachers say regularly that the package has filled a real gap in the market.

A number of students said that the interviewers were very poor and that training for admissions tutors in interview techniques would be useful. Some complained about poor organisation of interviews. Some claimed that the staff were not always fully conversant with the course syllabus and the options available.

Based on their interview experiences, the students gave a wide range of tips to future interviewees. The top tips are listed below:

(1) Be natural, friendly and open. Don't put on an "act".

(2) Be honest—if you don't know the answer don't try to bluff.

(3) Do not try to rehearse answers—a waste of time.

(4) Be prepared to argue and state your opinions.

(5) Ask questions such as "What is special about this course?" or "How many students will there be in my year?"

(6) Read the course descriptions in the prospectus before you go—know the course and the options available.

(7) Remember what you put on your UCCA/PCAS form: take a photocopy.

(8) Expect to be asked the three standard questions:
"Why do you want to do this subject?"
"Why here?" and,
"What A-levels/BTECs are you doing—what interests you most about those subjects?"

(9) Try to speak to current students on the course.

(10) Visit the halls of residence.

(11) Take a look at the campus and the town. Don't rush off to catch a train—use the rest of the day to do some detective work.

(12) Language students should expect to be interviewed in the language applied for. Music and Drama students usually have to audition. Creative subjects require evidence of achievement/portfolios, etc.

(13) Vocational courses may want to see commitment to the career/profession that the course is intended to lead to—particularly true for Teacher Training/Social Work, etc.

(14) Sandwich courses may want interviewees to demonstrate work skills and aptitude.

(15) Do not turn down the opportunity to attend an interview. Learn from the experience.

(16) Budget for interviews: they can be expensive in terms of travel costs.

(17) Some courses (particularly Humanities/Social Sciences) may have group discussions instead of the usual one-to-one interview. The intention is to judge the ability of applicants to express themselves.

(18) Some interviews include written tests.

(19) Be punctual but expect to be kept waiting.

(20) You are unlikely to be tested on your knowledge of the subject. It is more a test of aptitude, interest, the ability to think and to communicate.

Student Comments about Interviews

If you have the chance of an interview it is an opportunity to sell yourself. Even if you don't have the grades that are required, if you impress them they will take you anyway. (P)

We had two people interviewing, just normal conversation. Then he said "what would you do if you were reading a story in class and someone said that it was boring?" (BEd, C)

The interview wasn't at all what I had expected. The chap interviewing me had no knowledge of the area we were talking about. I was fearing there would be someone who knew absolutely everything. (U)

I went to one university under the assumption that it was an open day—I was grilled for half an hour. (U)

It was awful. I ended up talking to two eminent legal philosophers about whether murder was right or wrong, and whether anyone had the right to kill anyone else. I was 17 and pushed into a rather large corner. I emerged shaking. (U)

4.3   Induction and Familiarisation

The induction period effectively starts from the time that a place at the institution is confirmed. The questionnaire asked the students to rate their institution's induction procedures by giving a score out of ten. The focus groups were asked what information had been sent to them before their course actually started and, in retrospect, what additional information they would send to freshers.

Table 27   Rating for induction procedures for new students

Scale 1—10, 10 = excellent

	Average	Mode	Median
All	6.1	7	6
Polytechnics	6.0	5	6
Universities	6.3	7	6
Colleges	6.0	7	7

Overall, the students gave their institutions an average rating of 6.1 which would translate into "fair but could do better". The variations between individual institutions were considerable, indicating that some institutions take the induction process seriously whilst others leave freshers to fend for themselves. Overall, the universities scored slightly better than the other two sectors. This may be due to the fact that the PCFC sector has expanded so rapidly (compared with the universities) that admissions tutors now have too many freshers to service.

The focus groups were asked specifically about pre-enrolment information sent in the period between a place being confirmed and their actually starting the course. We attempted to discover what sort of information was sent, whether it was useful and finally what the students would ideally have liked to have received. Overall, 10% of the students said that the information sent to them was good or excellent, 40% said that it was OK and 50% had specific complaints to make about the quality or range of service that they had received.

Firstly, what sort of information do higher education institutions send to pre-enrolled students? The following items were mentioned most often:

reading lists, lists of accommodation, details of freshers' week events, registration details, lists of SU societies and clubs, course details, copy of the prospectus.

Induction—Bad Practice

The above list sounds fairly comprehensive but how useful was the information? Did it arrive at the right time and in a convenient format? In many cases the answer was a loud NO. Specific complaints were:

(a) Reading Lists

These were often long lists and too vague. Most titles were not easily obtainable. There was no indication as to which books were essential, useful, marginal, etc. Many were very expensive, yet no advice was given on whether to buy or borrow from the library. Many lists had not been up-dated for a number of years (the most recent texts were not included). Too much emphasis was placed on books/articles written by staff in the department or published by the institution.

(b) Accommodation

Too little information and too late. Parents and students worry a great deal about accommodation, yet confirmation of a place in a hall was far too long in coming. Lists of private accommodation were often out-of-date. In some cases all the places listed had been taken before the list had been received. No details were given of how far the accommodation was from the institution.

Those offered places in hall were often not told whether or not they were responsible for contents insurance, cooking equipment or bedding.

(c) Course Details

Most students start a course knowing about it only what was in the prospectus. In some cases this can be as little as 150 words. Only a small minority were sent a complete syllabus; a timetable for the first week (or longer); first-year options available (which they could discuss with friends and relatives); course leaflets, etc.

(d) Registration

Only one word described the students' response to registration—a fiasco. No-one seemed to know where to go, when or what to do when they arrived. Cases of lecturers not turning up were common. There was a lack of clear instructions and a map telling people where to go.

(e) Poor Co-ordination

Even those who had received good information complained about the lack of co-ordination. Too many offices seemed to be responsible for mailing information to new students: accommodation office, course admissions, counselling services, information offices, faculty officers, hall managers, registry, etc., not to mention the students' unions. Information arrived in dribs and drabs and there was an element of duplication.

(f) Information Explosion

Many students complained that too much was thrown at them on the first day: they were nervous and unsure of themselves. The whole freshers' week was too soon into the term and too intense.

(g) Students' Union

The union material was often criticised for being too glossy and for overselling what the union could provide. The freshers' week was thought to be too early in the first term. Many students said that they had made many bad decisions including joining societies which they never attended: this was expensive. The societies were "too hard sell". Some claimed that the union literature "gave the impression that the union ran the university".

We must remember that students' unions are easy targets for criticism. Perhaps the use of the title "union" is a mistake as it gives too much emphasis to their political activities?

Induction—Good Practice

There were many instances of good practice mentioned by the students. As indicated in the introduction, it is not our policy to name specific institutions. However, Durham University certainly won many plus marks from its students for the way in which they were welcomed by the institution. (We note in passing, and without passing judgement, that Durham University does not employ any student counsellors).

I was very impressed with the letters that I received before I came up. There were personal letters from the Principal, welcoming me to the College, and information on what was going to happen when I arrived— so I felt really wanted. We have interviewee reps and freshers' reps in the college who wrote personal letters too. I was so impressed—someone inviting me to coffee in her room, which is excellent.

I think the personal touch of undergraduates writing and inviting you for coffee is quite comforting—you don't feel quite so lost.

My College sent me an information book containing information on every aspect of College life.

I had a letter from one of the students in College...drop round, ring up, write to me if you're worried, etc.

The experience of these students was very positive. These first impressions will stand the University in good stead for many years.

The following are examples of good practice and ideas for induction procedures/information as cited by the students in the focus groups. They are grouped into three sections: before the student arrives, the first day, and the first week. The students clearly felt that the needs of freshers change over these periods.

(a) Before the Fresher Arrives

(i)   *The personal letter*

The letter confirming the place on the course should be a personal one and should be signed by either the course leader or the head of department using first names if at all possible (e.g. Dr Alan Jones).

(ii) *The co-ordinated information booklet*

All other information required by new entrants should accompany the letter or be forwarded within a week. All information should be sent in one package, so as to be co-ordinated.

The unco-ordinated approach was considered to be very unprofessional. Rather than various parts of the institution producing "scrappy leaflets", many students suggested that the general information should be brought together into one booklet— "Welcome to XYZ institution—a guide for new students."

It was suggested that students should be involved in the compilation of this booklet (perhaps as part of the enterprise initiative) as they know exactly what new students need to know. It was also suggested that this publication should include information about the students' union, rather than separate information being provided.

It was recognised that a separate booklet for each faculty would be required to give more specific information which could not be contained in the general publication.

The information that the students felt was necessary at the pre-entry stage and should be included in a general booklet was:

A map of the town/city.

Local places of interest.

A plan of the campus/college buildings, showing where the nearest cash-points/banks are located, students' union, refectory, halls of residence, car parks to be used by new arrivals, etc.

A college calendar giving important events (term dates, etc.).

A list/details of union societies/clubs with contact information.

Accommodation information to include:

> The policy for allocating hall places, e.g. when the entrant can expect to have a place confirmed;

> Details of what cooking equipment, bedding, etc., is required;

> Cost of halls (what is included);

> An indication of average prices, a guide to tenant/landlord "issues" and where to get advice, and for those requiring private accommodation, information on insurances.

Information about public transport routes/prices/special discount cards.

Finances: how to budget, grants, loans and a brief guide to welfare benefits.

The faculty-specific booklet should contain the following:

A plan showing the location of the department, indicating the place where students should go on the first day.

A timetable for the first week, and one for the regular term. This should indicate when any field trip weeks would take place.

A reading list. This should be very short and should only include books that are widely available in shops/libraries throughout the UK. If the institution library has copies, the list should say that purchasing books is not necessary.

Photographs and pen portraits of first-year tutors.

A detailed course structure explaining exactly what each unit includes.

For modular courses a clear explanation of the options available (so that entrants can have time to think through their electives with advice from friends and relatives, and without the pressures of freshers' week).

An indication of any study materials that students will need to purchase (particularly relevant for Art, Design, etc.).

Details of when and where registration/induction will take place and what students should bring with them (passport photograph, etc.).

(b)   The First Day

The first day of term should include organised induction. This "event" should include:

A welcome from the head of department.

Registration/enrolment.

A informal meeting with staff.

The opportunity to talk to second-year students.

A tour of the department.

An introduction from a students' union representative.

Following the Durham University model, new students could be paired with a second-year student, particularly for the first week. Some suggested that the student should, if possible, come from the same area of the country as the new entrant.

(c)   The First Week

The first week of the new term should include the following:

A talk by a librarian specialising in the student's subject of study.

Optional study skills sessions.

A talk by a student counsellor (many said that they would not seek advice from someone they had not even seen before).

A sale of second-hand books and other study materials.

Many students suggested that the freshers' fair should not be held in the first week of term but late in the second week, once students had "found their feet".

Student comments about induction

I got about 10 sheets of paper when I registered. It would have been useful to have got the information earlier. (U)

This University is very good for sending things out. They sent me decent information which was one of the deciding factors of coming here. (U)

Nobody seemed to know what was going on during the first day registration. They could have given a detailed plan, a timetable perhaps, with a few fixed times and places to be at. (U)

The registration was a fiasco. (U)

I didn't make the grades to get here so they said I could take a year off and that they would contact me the summer before I came here. I heard nothing. I 'phoned them and they hadn't got a clue who I was! (U)

Do this, do that. No explanation as to how to do it. (U)

I wanted to know about accommodation sooner. (U)

I had a reading list which amounted to £400 worth of books which was a load of rubbish. All the books you will need the second-years will sell them you when you arrive. You don't need half of them. (U)

51

The History Society sent me a reading list of what was really needed. They cut the list down. (U)

I didn't realise you could get course leaflets. They didn't mention them in the prospectus. (U)

I read the reading list but not the books. Not needed. (U)

As a mature student with a family I didn't receive notification that I hadn't got accommodation until six weeks before the course started. We had to move from Somerset and there was no guarantee that we could sort things out in time. This service was very bad. (U)

They should co-operate between departments and the Union. (U)

My parents moved in the summer and they sent all the information to our old address. I had informed them we were moving and the new address. It was a real hassle. (U)

I would have liked something with pictures and names of staff. I still haven't got a clue who some of them are. (U)

The lecturers tend to recommend their own books. (U)

I was deluged with information. We got a reading list but the second-years had told us not to get any of them. It is very useful to talk to second-years. (U)

They sent me a reading list and I went out and bought and read the whole lot. I never actually used one of the books they told me to buy. (U)

I got a personal letter before the UCCA slip. That really influenced me. (U)

I knew nothing about the course before I started. There was such a wide range of options. I was advised by my personal tutor on enrolment day to take these particular subjects. He knows best, so I took them and hated them. (U)

I was sent a vague summer reading list. Some of them were totally irrelevant. On the whole it tended to worry people who thought they perhaps should have read them all. (U)

I did have a reading list and I got them from the library. I couldn't get past the first few pages. It almost put me off going altogether. (P)

They didn't send me anything at all—except a chaplaincy leaflet! I had to find accommodation with no help at all. (P)

I got this red students' union guide which I wish I had earlier. (P)

I think there should be a practical guide about living in a flat or house. How to cook on a small budget. (P)

They should send information to all students. Some got it, some didn't. (P)

I think they should send a complete list of how to get accommodation, where you should go, how much to expect to pay and what sort of contract you should have with the landlord. (P)

They sent me accommodation details, also a diary, a good pub guide and maps with useful telephone numbers on them. (P)

We were sort of dumped here on the first day and we didn't know what we were doing. I think my course was dropped by 19 in the first year. Not very well organised. (P)

I was sent a full pack. It told you where everything was. Very helpful. (P)

They sent me a reading list. I went and bought and read the whole lot and never actually used one of them. I had to go and sell them to a foolish first year. Don't take any notice of reading lists. (U)

They did neglect to tell us about one subject which all students hate. It's useless and wastes six hours a week. (C)

It wasn't until a week before term that they told me I had a place in halls. . . I got mine two weeks before and I was panicking and phoning up. It was just the same for the second-year. . . . The same happened to me as well. . . . Ten days before the start of term they told me there wasn't room in halls. I had one week to find somewhere to live. (All at the same college)

The details about accommodation didn't come for weeks. My parents were not impressed. They panicked. (C)

They just said "read a few books on economics!". (C)

I got all the information within ten days. I thought that was very good. We had a freshers' briefing—that took away the panic. Very helpful. (C)

We had to choose between halls and college houses. I had never seen them or been told the difference. (C)

I found that I bought books that were in the library anyway. (C)

The induction day was very boring. We sat around for hours listening to these people droning on about things we knew nothing about. (C)

I got an accommodation list which was all out-of-date by the time I got it. (C)

You were lucky. I didn't get any accommodation information, I kept phoning up. (C)

I wasn't sent anything. They even lost my exam results. (C)

They said to take £50 for freshers' week as it was expensive. You join clubs and it's £10 to join the Union. I spent £150. (C)

There is a second-hand bookshop here but I only found it by chance. (C)

They should think about what they send out rather than saying "we always send this". (C)

As far as accommodation was concerned I was just told to turn up on the day! (C)

I had little time after clearing but I promptly got details about accommodation, reading list, etc. (C)

The day I arrived I found out where I was going to stay! (C)

As a mature student I had expected a list of child minders in the area. I phoned up but they were always too busy to speak to me. (C)

They fixed a place for me to live, sent me lots of information. They like to be nice to foreigners (a comment from an overseas student). (C)

4.4 Transition into Higher Education

The focus groups were asked to discuss whether they thought FE college, school or sixth-form was a good preparation for higher education. The students identified several factors which they felt were central to successful transition into higher education. The clear message from the students was that those who found the transition into higher education to be relatively smooth (both academically and socially) were those who had previously attended schools or colleges with similar regimes in terms of the nature and organisation of study, the atmosphere of the organisation, and, the staff/student relationship.

There were clear differences between those who had previously studied BTEC qualifications or A-levels, and between those who had attended different types of school or college.

(a) BTEC or A-level

Those students who had done BTEC qualifications were very positive about their education and claimed that the transition to higher education had been very smooth. These former BTEC students felt that they had had a distinct advantage over A-level students in the first year irrespective of whether they were on degree or HND courses. Many claimed that the first year was easier than the final year of the BTEC National Diploma.

BTEC students cited the fact that they were more used to independent learning than their A-level counterparts. They were used to researching their own work, using libraries and working on real projects rather than essays. They claimed that higher education's emphasis on discussions, team-work and continuous assessment was what they were used to.

Previous research shows that BTEC students tend to get poorer results in their degrees than A-level students; so are these former BTEC students wrong? BTEC is often chosen at 16 by those with less academic ability: it is perhaps likely that the natural academic ability of A-level students comes to the fore as the degree course progresses (perhaps this does not augur well for the Government's proposals for vocational qualifications at 18 +). However, in terms of the transitional phase, BTEC methods seem to be successful.

Some A-level students were critical of their courses, particularly their reliance on final examinations. They felt that they had acquired few study skills. However, former BTEC students did feel that the A-level students had developed better essay skills.

We found virtually no students who had entered through the BTEC route who had anything negative to say about their previous education. Many A-level students were very dismissive of the nature of their sixth-form studies. Many saw them only as a means to an end; the end being grades to enter higher education. Some BTEC students did complain that HE staff treated them as second class, although this wasn't widespread.

Student Comments

I think that A-levels are pretty bad really. They are ridiculous exams. . . . You have got to write about four novels in three hours. (English A-level)

In A-levels you just write down the facts. No chance to use your imagination at all.

I don't think my course is any different to BTEC.

My BTEC doesn't relate to my Law degree. Here you have six months to do an essay!

The way of working in BTEC is very similar to our degree. I would have found it very hard to go from A-levels to this.

A-levels are totally different from HND. You are assessed here and things are explained at the end of it.

BTEC is a better preparation.

A-levels are constructed for you. Here you have to work for yourself.

A-levels just concentrate on regurgitating facts and figures. You don't learn how to think.

*I was excellently prepared because the HND runs on very smoothly and I knew exactly what to expect. It is mostly A-level students who have problems as it's so different. BTECs are **very good**.*

BTEC is excellent. It gives you a real advantage over A-level people. They come here and it's different.

BTEC is excellent. I wouldn't do a degree if it wasn't for employers' attitudes. I don't think you learn any more in the extra time you need to do a degree over an HND.

My comprehensive school was a good preparation for here. You passed the exams despite your teachers not because of them.

No real problems. I did BTEC and it has run straight on.

University is much harder than BTEC but we did have the right sort of method. A good preparation.

Scottish Highers are a bit like lectures but I spent the first year catching up here.

(b) School Type

Students who had been at tertiary, FE or sixth-form colleges felt that the atmosphere there was similar to higher education in terms of staff attitudes, e.g. the need to organise personal time, the more adult environment, etc. FE colleges were certainly very well thought of by their alumni and were perceived as being "a good bridge between school and higher education". There was more emphasis on self-discipline, uniforms were not compulsory and students' needs were given more priority than those of parents. The FE colleges also had mature students and this was cited as something useful which schools did not offer.

Conversely, independent schools seemed to have produced a resentful set of students. These schools were seen as being authoritarian. The students felt ill-prepared socially for higher education. Boarding schools were seen as helping students to gain independence from home and many mentioned that they had learned some domestic and life skills there. Grammar schools were described as "exam factories". Single sex schools were criticised by all the interviewees who had attended them. However, our sample of such students was very small.

Student Comments

You learn a lot from mature people. School didn't have them.

I was at public school. No preparation at all.

57

My sixth-form was totally irrelevant and useless. Very traditional —the sixth-form was just like the rest of the school. It was a girls' grammar school with 11+. I had a very low opinion of myself when I left.

I went to an all-girls' grammar school. There was far too much formality between staff and pupils, even to the extent of punishment for sixth-formers. The attitude of most staff was unreasonable. I took a year off and went to an FE college—the atmosphere there was totally different, very informal and I got on very well.

My sixth-form was very structured and formal. The discipline was good but it didn't prepare me to take responsibility for myself.

The leap was a very big one. I wasn't ready for it. I went to an all-boys' school.

The system of teaching is completely different at boarding school. We were spoon-fed and punished if we didn't do things. There were rules and regulations for absolutely everything. Here the lecturers try to put you on the same level as them. I was expecting lectures where you sit down and take loads of notes. In fact it's a lot of group work. If you don't work you fail.

I think school is a good preparation. I was so used to being pushed to get my work done that I went on in the same habit.

School is not a good preparation. I don't know whether it is lack of teacher encouragement to do things for yourself or whether it's the attitude you have at that age. We were too spoon-fed.

At school you don't have to use your initiative enough.

At my sixth-form college I was free and independent. Like here really.

I am glad that I went to FE college to do my A-levels. We had to fend for ourselves more than at school.

The school wasn't good preparation—too much discipline and the uniform. It was a boarding school so I did learn to live away from home and to organise myself to some extent. At school you had to study two hours a night and were told what to write.

FE college is good; school isn't. You begin to take your own responsibility at college which you don't at school.

Schools are just A-level factories.

The whole teaching atmosphere is much more mature than at school. You are on first name terms with lecturers.

Schools protect you too much. Everything was compulsory. Here it's all voluntary.

I was at a big comprehensive which was good because you got used to the large numbers of people.

A great number of the students claimed that they had been ill-prepared for higher education in terms of the study-skills required such as private reading, note-taking, time management, asking questions in big groups, team/project work, information retrieval using IT systems, etc.

Many students complained that at school and FE colleges they were not encouraged to read enough—for study or pleasure. In higher education they were expected to do much more reading and many found this difficult.

Classes in higher education were generally seen as being much larger than for A-levels. Many complained that they felt unable to ask questions in such large groups. Some university students felt that lectures were very formal. Many found note-taking very difficult in the first year. Skills such as note-taking were assumed, yet most had not had to take them at such speed because schools gave hand-outs and teachers could be interrupted if the student had "missed something".

Few students had been introduced to microfiche or computer-held data in school libraries. Using such materials was a problem to some new higher education students.

Schools were perceived not to be introducing enough project or team work, and pupils were not encouraged to challenge the information presented to them.

School life was seen as very organised with a very full timetable. Higher education has very little time-tabled work. Many students found this difficult to handle as they had developed few time management skills. Conversely some (fewer) students did say that the discipline of the school timetable had helped them to get into a routine of working so many hours a week.

Student Comments

You have to learn to read systematically if you want to do well.

Reading is very, very important.

They should encourage people to read more at school.

They don't prepare you well at school for a degree. It's different —you have to do lots of reading here.

They should help you with note-taking techniques. It can be difficult.

Some lecturers give you hand-outs, others just rattle on and you have to go away and find out what on earth they were talking about.

At school I was taught. Here there are very few times when someone is actually teaching you.

You have to learn how to use the extra time—there is so much of it.

No-one instructs you on how to organise and use your time—it is all assumed.

O-levels are spoon-fed. A-levels make you do some things for yourself. For a degree you have to do it all yourself.

Where I went you were made to work, whereas here it's up to you. If you are trained to work then that's a good preparation.

You are pushed to work at school. Here you have to push yourself.

This course is much easier than A-levels. So much free time.

Here I'm not prone to going to the library: I tend to sit around in the coffee bar and think I can do it all later. It catches up with you. At school you worked and chatted. Here it's just chat.

At school the classes were 6—10. Here it's 100+. You can't ask questions.

Here the classes are much bigger and to ask questions isn't the done thing.

Here the university lectures are so formal. You can't ask questions or interrupt. In FE there was much more discussion and smaller groups.

Here you are encouraged not to agree with the mainstream but to have your own angle.

Here you can ask questions. In school you just took notes.

The jump from O to A-levels is a shock. Higher education is something of a relief.

The step from A-level to degree isn't very big at all.

Teaching in school is much better than here.

Social life has an affect on your work. I didn't drink before.

The HND is different to school. More based on seminars and vocational. We never get a lecturer who stands up there and reads off paragraph after paragraph.

My FE college was like here except we didn't have the very big lectures.

There is no comparison. I just used to coast at school. I used to love it because I did nothing. Here you feel a sense of vocation.

Generally, students with a background in FE, and who had taken the BTEC route, were much happier than A-level sixth-form students in virtually every respect. Socially and academically they felt that their previous experiences had proved to be a good foundation and that transition into higher education had posed few problems.

A-levels were not perceived very positively. They did not encourage the development of the study skills most frequently needed in higher education: team work, independent study, planning, notetaking, report writing, and debate. This suggests that A-levels should perhaps cease to be arid academic challenges. They should instead concentrate on team building and communication skills, such as those expected in infant and primary schools, GCSEs, higher education and employment.

On the positive side, those in Humanities subjects did feel that A-levels were good for learning the art of essay-writing. A-levels did allow students to specialise in certain subjects and many with A-levels felt that the standard of the first-year of a degree was similar or below that to which they had become accustomed.

4.5 Amount of Study

Many students found it difficult to adapt to the amount of "free time" available in higher education compared with their previous experiences in school or FE college, where most of the periods were time-tabled. Not only did the amount of free time create difficulties in terms of time management and motivation, but it also led many of the respondents to conclude that higher education was "easy" because it was less pressurised than A-levels, less intense. The general atmosphere was very relaxed.

A good number of the students who took part in the discussions felt that higher education was too unstructured and too "student centred". The focus group participants were asked how much time they had spent studying during the past seven days. The average (including lectures, seminars and private study) was 27 hours a week, within a range of 6 to 60. On average, Engineering students spent the greatest time studying, with practical "lab sessions" being an important element of their first-year studies. Drama and Music students also seemed to work relatively long hours. Students on Humanities and desk-based courses tended to study the least number of hours. The exception were English students who had to read a great deal, although many saw this as much as recreation as work.

University students tended, on average, to work fewer hours. Far more university students tended to do very little (less than 15 hours a week). Might one argue that it is not the quantity of time expended but how effectively the time is used?

Many of the students who were not doing many hours felt guilty. They found it difficult to motivate themselves. Some felt that the institution was to blame because the lecturers took little interest and did not push them enough. Institutions, they claimed, should discriminate more and realise that not all students are self-starters.

The idea of a more intense two-year degree might well appeal to some of these Humanities-type students. Many actually suggested a shorter degree course because they were wasting time and getting into debt whilst doing so. Most HND students interviewed felt that the extra year for a degree was a waste of time and that they learned more in two years than their friends had done in three. Some students said that there was a culture of doing very little work in their department.

The questionnaire asked students whether the volume of work relating to their course was more or less than they had expected. Most students opted for the "as expected" box, but more claimed to be working longer than expected than vice versa as shown in **Table 28**.

Table 28   Volume of work on the course

	All%	P%	U%	C%
More than expected	33	31	34	32
As expected	48	50	45	50
Less than expected	19	19	21	18

These figures seem, at first glance, to be at odds with the results of the focus groups. However, the students in the focus groups revealed very low levels of expectation when it came to study hours. Many who were working 20 hours or less claimed that it was more than they had expected to do before they started the course.

It's more than I expected—but I do the extra.

I do 30 hours a week. It is a great deal more than I expected.

I ought to do 30 but it's more like 20.

I fit it in when I can (!)—about 25.

24. I don't count weekends because I have a job then. More than I had expected.

Eight hours a week. I do some reading for seminars if I have them. A lot less than I had expected.

I have less than an hour a day in lectures but I have orchestra and practice sessions. About 50 hours a week which is what I had expected.

It's difficult to pin down when you're working and when you aren't. Sometimes when you are lying in bed and you have got an essay to do the next week you can be thinking about the main points that you need to get across. There are a lot of hours when I'm thinking about my course. (Perhaps this student feels able to count the content of dreams as part of her workload?)

35 hours a week. What I expected but still a shock.

18 hours a week—more than I expected (and intended).

60 hours a week. I have been told that I am working a little too hard. I was terrified by my low A-level grades.

30 and definitely more!

12 hours—just about right I think.

63 a week. I play two instruments and there's five hours practice a day.

To test this issue further, Heist questioned 603 students in sixth-forms and FE colleges nation-wide (May 1991) and asked them "how many hours per week would you expect to work during the first year of higher education (including lectures, seminars and private study)?" The average was 32.4 hours per week—well in excess of what most students appear to be working.

The results from **Table 26** have been broken-down by subject area. The results basically support the comments of the focus groups in terms of identifying which subjects appear to require the most number of hours of study per week. The subjects where the greatest numbers of students claimed to be doing longer hours than anticipated were Engineering/Technology, Built Environment, and Science/Maths.

Chapter 5   The Student as a Consumer

5.1   Introduction

In this chapter we examine students' opinions of their institutions and their courses. How do they rate their institution's services and facilities, the students' union, the quality of the course, etc. We asked if they would recommend their institution or course.

By examining the questionnaire results in conjunction with the findings from the focus groups, one important technical conclusion can be drawn: students who claim they would recommend their course or institution should not be confused with satisfied students. Even students with a large number of complaints are still, surprisingly, likely to recommend. One student who claimed that he would very definitely recommend his course then spent five minutes explaining what was wrong with it.

Why are (partially) dissatisfied students still likely to provide courses/institutions with recommendations?

(a) Most students are "having a good time" socially and this tends to compensate for most deficiencies in the course/institution.

(b) The great majority of students have no experience of other higher education courses/institutions with which to compare their own—they therefore tend to assume that their course, with all its faults, is OK.

(c) Most courses/institutions make sure that students are aware of institution success stories. We noted several comments such as "our department says it is the best in the country".

(d) Students validate their own decisions: few are willing to admit that they chose to go to a poor institution or are on a poor course.

(e) The "football supporter syndrome". In the company of fellow students from the same institution undergraduates are openly critical about specific aspects of their course/ institution—in the same way as football supporters on the terraces are critical of their manager/players.

However, when asked about their team by outsiders, they tend to be more positive (it may have weaknesses but it is still better than the opposition). Students appear to have a similar psychology, taking on the role of college supporter.

When students were asked to rate their institution on an overall basis, the results were consistently higher than when the students were asked to rate particular aspects of the institution. On one level they are the supporter, on another a more critical consumer.

5.2 Opinions of the College

The students were asked in an open question to identify what they considered to be the worst aspect of their host institution. The most frequent answers are listed below in **Table 29**. Remember that these are not what the students think are simply bad aspects, but the worst.

Table 29   What is the worst aspect of your institution?

All mentions to an open question

	All%	P%	U%	C%
Organisation/administration	11	14	6	14
Atmosphere/student mix	10	6	16	8
Poor facilities	7	7	3	10
Housing/accommodation	7	9	8	5
Buildings/site	6	9	7	3
Lecturers/staff	5	3	4	7
Students' union	5	7	7	4
Overcrowding	5	7	3	5
Social/sports	5	3	7	6
Canteen	4	4	3	5
Isolated location	4	1	5	5
Split site	3	7	1	2
Amount of work	3	1	4	3
Library	3	4	3	3

Others mentioned were cost of living, the course, poor reputation, overworked lecturers, security and lighting, lack of funds for the college, size of the institution.

The most frequent response was "poor organisation and administration". This was the top answer for both polytechnics and colleges but much less of an issue with university students. The "atmosphere/student mix" (social class or ethnic) was considered the most pressing problem by university students.

For polytechnic students the conditions of the buildings and the lack of student accommodation were highly rated problems, whilst 10% of college students complained about poor facilities in general.

The students were then asked, in another open question, to rate the best aspect of their institution (**Table 30**). The "good atmosphere" was rated top by students in all three sectors, and particularly by college students (31%)—perhaps reflecting the smaller size of the colleges and their more intimate nature.

The course was placed second, with particular emphasis given by polytechnic respondents (14%). Students seem to appreciate the quality of their environment. University undergraduates are particularly keen on the social life.

Table 30   The best aspects of your institution

All mentions to an open question

	All%	P%	U%	C%
Atmosphere	25	15	23	31
Course	12	14	11	12
Environment	10	10	11	9
Quality of staff	8	9	6	8
Social life	7	9	10	4
Academic facilities	7	9	6	5
Staff/student relations	6	7	4	7
Size	3	2	6	3

Others mentioned were sporting facilities, library, reputation, students' union and students.

As **Table 31** indicates, the great majority of students (87%) said that they would recommend their institution to someone considering higher education. University students were the most likely to recommend (92%) and they were also more definite in their recommendation (54%). College students were the least firm in their support, although the actual figures were still very high.

Table 31   Would you recommend your college to someone considering higher education?

	All%	P%	U%	C%
Yes definitely	42	42	54	31
	}87	}86	}92	}83
Yes—some reservations	45	44	38	52
Uncertain	8	9	5	10
No	4	3	2	5
Definitely not	1	1	1	2
No response	0	1	0	0

A series of questions then asked the undergraduates to rate various aspects of their institution on a scale of 1—10, with 10 being excellent. The average scores are presented in Table 32 and they help us to highlight some of the strengths and weaknesses of the three sectors.

Table 32   Satisfaction with specific aspects of the institution

Average rating on scale of 1—10 (10 = excellent)

	All	P	U	C
Library/learning resources	7.12	6.99	7.73	6.58
Computing/IT support	6.26	6.57	6.38	5.93
Sporting facilities	5.93	5.50	6.87	5.28
Social clubs	5.92	6.25	6.67	4.95
Bars/catering	5.67	5.63	6.26	5.10
Private study facilities	5.58	5.71	5.68	5.41
Entertainment	5.40	5.38	5.94	4.87
Students' union	5.19	4.97	5.48	5.06
Overall average	5.90	5.90	6.34	5.45

Librarians will rejoice at being placed top in terms of satisfaction in all three sectors. Libraries scored particularly well in the university sector where facilities are generally good and resources per FTE much higher than in the PCFC funded institutions.

We explored the question of student satisfaction relating specifically to the availability of library books in more detail. During the coffee bar discussions we asked the students to rate this aspect of their institution on a scale of 1—4 where 1 was excellent and 4 poor. The sample was 2,400 and unlike the other parts of the research, included students from all years. The results broadly support the findings in **Table 32** with universities being rated at 2.2, polytechnics at 2.3 and colleges at 2.4. We must remember that we are measuring satisfaction, not absolute quality. In the opinion of the researcher conducting the interviews, the real difference between the three sectors is much more marked. The students, however, have little or no comparative knowledge.

The discussions did reveal that satisfaction drops considerably as students progress through their courses. First-year students gave a rating of 2.1, second and third-years a rating of 2.4 and fourth-years 2.6. As the students mature they appear to become more critical. This may be due to the increasing demands of the course or the fact that work in the later stages is more vital to their final degree classification.

The polytechnics scored well in terms of computing and IT support, whilst the universities' more palatial sporting facilities showed through in these figures.

The results are disappointing for the colleges, with social and entertainment facilities being rated as rather poor. Students' unions fared poorly also.

Overall the scores are no more than "average" yet in spite of these modest assessments, 87% of the sample would still recommend their institution.

Comments from the Focus Groups

The following comments were made during the focus groups to the same open question: "What are the best and worst aspects of your college?" The following examples illustrate the main themes and issues that were raised. In some cases, such as whether the campus is quiet and isolated or bustling and city based, it is a case of one man's meat being another man's poison.

Social life/Atmosphere

The best thing is the social life. The worst thing is getting up in the morning after the social life and counting your pennies to see if you can afford a black coffee. (C)

69

Being white is a problem here—not many societies are geared to white people's needs, more towards Asians. (P)

People on Physics degrees are not that popular, but you do manage to make some outside friends. (P)

The worst thing here is the social life. In university there are 101 clubs to join but here you feel as though you know everyone within the first month. (C)

You meet people from all over the place. I'm from Lancashire and it was nice to meet some southerners! (U)

The best thing is the homely college atmosphere—the worst thing is being intimidated by certain lecturers. (U)

The sex ratio (gender balance) is a bit strange. (C)

It's difficult to mix with anyone outside of your course. (C)

The best thing are the students—they are the worst thing too. You get the stereo-type who is arrogant and doesn't care about ordinary people. (U)

This is a no nonsense place. I came from Cambridge which is full of yuppy idiots—screaming left and screaming right! (U)

The best thing is friends. The worst thing is that on an isolated campus everything is so expensive. (U)

The worst thing is that the locals are unfriendly towards the students. The local lads are very violent. (U)

The place is very cliquey—the worst thing. (U)

I can't stand the middle class cliques—you get them in halls and clubs. (U)

The local people resent the students. (P)

The city is geared up for students. You don't get enough chance to mix with people in other departments. (P)

The Campus/Area

The worst thing is the area—not a lot going on! (C)

The Polytechnic is on three sites and I don't like the travelling. (P)

It's too spread out and can be awful if your course is on several sites. (P)

The situation is lovely and you get to know everyone really well. In a big institution you get lost. (C)

It costs 75p each way into town. (C)

It's quiet which is good and bad. I come from a rural area and you get more chance to work. It can be a bit boring. (C)

The friends are terrific. The concrete campus is depressing. (U)

The best thing is London, the worst the lack of friendliness. (C)

The worst thing is that the College is split up and you don't know others around the College. (C)

With hindsight I would have preferred being in the middle of a city —it's quite cut-off here. (U)

The worst thing is that I miss the countryside. (U)

Best is the freedom. The town is the pits. (C)

The town itself is the worst thing—it's atrocious. The university is friendly. (U)

It's a lovely campus but it seems to rain a lot here. (U)

The car parking is appalling. (P)

It's a very pretty campus. The worst thing is that you see students all the time and it's a very artificial community. (U)

Course-Related

The best aspect is the course. My guitar teacher really is the best. (C)

71

The flexibility of the course is the best. (C)

I really like my course. The worst thing is finance. (C)

The lecturers are all so helpful. The resources of the College are awful. (C)

The worst thing is the lack of guidance—you're just left on your own. (U)

The lectures are like verbal text books. They cannot teach—it's pathetic! (U)

I don't like the big projects because you don't get any help. (P)

Organisation/Communication

A lack of communication between tutors and students. It is difficult to get them to listen to your ideas. (C)

The lecturers are really friendly and you can have great fun. (C)

There are twice as many students as last year and no more lecturers. We have to do evening lectures. (C)

The worst thing is the organisation. Also the attitude of some lecturers. If they show disrespect to the students they'll get disrespect back. (P)

French last year was very disorganised—we were all very unhappy. (P)

Sport/Canteen/Students' Union/Entertainment

College meals are the worst! (C)

The best thing is the cheap beer in the bar. (C)

The union is rubbish. The entertainment is not good. (C)

The canteen is very expensive but the sports facilities are good. (C)

There are good "dos" and sports. All the first-years have nowhere to live—they are in caravans in the car park. (C)

It's a nice students' bar and stuff but we can't get access to college equipment on our course. (C)

There are lots of foreign students here which is good. The worst thing is that it is too far from Tottenham Hotspur Football Club. (U)

The best thing is the women's rugby team. (P)

Miscellaneous

The best thing is not having any parents here. The worst thing is the American students. (U)

The worst thing is the lack of females in the halls. (P)

If you don't get into halls in the first year I think you feel as though you've missed out. (P)

I think that lack of money is part of the adventure. The facilities here are not very good. (P)

5.3 Opinions of Courses

A similar set of questions were posed in relation to course satisfaction. Students were asked if they would recommend their course to someone considering studying in that subject area. Again, the vast majority (88%) said that they would, as shown in **Table 33**. On this occasion, the colleges fare better and it is the universities that have the weakest level of support (albeit at a very high level).

Table 33   Would you recommend your courses to someone considering studying in your subject area?

	All%	P%	U%	C%
Yes definitely	47	49	44	49
	}88	}87	}87	}89
Yes—some reservations	41	38	43	40
Uncertain	7	7	7	6
No	3	3	3	2
Definitely not	1	1	2	1
No response	1	2	1	2

In **Table 33(a)** we give the results by subject area which show that Teacher Training courses appear to have the largest army of supporters with 92% claiming that they would recommend their course. Engineering and Technology courses received the weakest response. We know that drop-out rates in this area are relatively high.

Table 33(a) Students likely to recommend course by subject area

Subject Area	%
Education/Teacher Training	93
Humanities/Social Science	92
Built Environment	90
Science/Mathematics	89
Art/Design/Music/Drama	89
Health/Social Services	88
IT/Computing	88
Business/Law	87
Engineering/Technology	84

Table 34 gives overall ratings for specific aspects of courses and suggests that students are generally more satisfied with their courses than with their institutions as a whole.

Polytechnics were rated more highly for quality of lecturing and for student participation in course development. This will be gratifying for the polytechnics which are generally considered to be teaching rather than research organisations. It will be interesting to see whether the levels of satisfaction with teaching in universities will be raised in the future as many begin to lose their research base and develop more along the lines of teaching institutions.

The "coffee bar" discussions also asked students whether they were satisfied with the quality of instruction from staff. The ratings for each sector were very close but once again a clear trend appeared with a poorer rating given as the students progressed through each year.

The universities scored well for resources and for organisation, whilst the colleges gained the best results for personal support and for communication between staff and students.

The average scores are very similar for all three sectors, as too were the students' ratings for "overall learning experience". It is again interesting to note that the average rating for the components of the courses (6.38) was considerably lower than the rating for the more general notion of overall learning experience (7.25).

Table 34   Satisfaction with aspects of the course

Average rating on a scale 1—10 (10 = excellent)

	All	**P**	**U**	**C**
Subject content	7.28	7.31	7.43	7.11
Quality of lecturing	6.74	6.85	6.70	6.72
Personal support	6.50	6.34	6.41	6.69
Communication with staff	6.47	5.68	6.53	6.93
Resources/equipment	6.31	6.11	6.62	6.14
Organisation/efficiency	5.88	5.53	6.52	5.47
Student participation	5.53	5.81	5.17	5.71
Average	6.38	6.23	6.48	6.39
Overall learning experience	7.25	7.22	7.27	7.24

Comments from the Focus Groups

It was remarkable how many students criticised their course, or elements of it (sometimes in very damning tones) yet still said that they would recommend it.

A number of issues were raised by most groups across all three sectors. They were:

New Courses

These were often criticised for being disorganised and unco-ordinated.

It was a new course. It was awful—so badly organised. The timetable was really spread-out. We spend too much time on Europe which was not as the course title said. I would recommend it. (P)

Modular/Joint Honours

Such courses were often seen as unco-ordinated, poorly organised and lacking proper communication between staff and students in different departments or on different sites. A constant criticism was "lack of depth": students felt that they were taking a large number of subjects at no more than A-level standard. They expected more rigour from higher education. Joint honours students complained about being expected to reach single honours standards in both subjects. They also had to buy two sets of books or materials.

My course is modular and the courses are bought-in. It needs much better co-ordination. (U)

It is a modular course which is good. There is a lack of communication between the sites and departments. Nobody who teaches me Sociology knows that I am doing Educational Studies. The personal tutor is busy and hard to find. It wouldn't be any good for someone who needed encouragement and personal support. I would recommend it but you have to sort out problems for yourself and be resilient. (P)

The problem areas are where we have inputs from other departments. There is a lack of co-ordination or just their nature doesn't fit in with others. (U)

I would prefer to study subjects in more depth. (C)

It was all too general—no depth. (C)

I am enjoying it—the only thing is that the first year was very disjointed. I felt cheated because I was studying more subjects than at A-level. It ended up as combined studies. It was meant to be Politics. (U)

Watch out for joint honours courses—mine is a complete mess. Fortunately the Biotechnology Department is well-organised so I would recommend it. (U)

History and Sociology is really good. The problem is that they are in two departments and you're neither here nor there. (U)

It's OK. The two subjects together—there's a lot of overlap. (P)

It's a broad-based course, you cover a lot of subjects shallowly we don't get any depth. (P)

Doing a BEd we share work with the Geography department. Because of the modular system the timetable changes each week. I have been told not to worry if I miss some lectures which is wrong. (C)

Irrelevant Subjects

A number of students complained about modules which appeared to have little in common with the course as a whole. Accounting and Computing were cited most often. The students felt that they were in the syllabus because they were fashionable "in" subjects. Optional subjects were welcomed.

Some sessions appear pointless but I'm told that all will become clear at the end of the third year. (U)

I am satisfied but this year only a third of the options were History—a third were Computing! They should not be in our course. (U)

In the first year we had some subjects that were totally irrelevant to Business Studies. The Computing lectures were useless—too technical and confusing.(P)

Languages

Many courses now include Languages—often as an option. This was viewed positively but there were practical problems in delivering the courses because of the variation in competence amongst the students. Some had A-level, others were complete beginners. Those with advanced skills felt that they were not progressing. Some wanted the language tuition to be more relevant to the main subject—e.g. French for lawyers or Business Spanish.

Language options are good but everyone is on a different level. They need a foundation so that we are all on the same level. (P)

Lecturers

The quality of lecturers was perceived as being very variable. Most were good but a minority were thought to be very bad indeed. Many students felt that colleges should be more tough with poor lecturers. Others felt that lecturing/teaching skills were lacking, particularly in the university sector. Recent research (4) has drawn attention to the fact that new entrants to the teaching profession in higher education have been left to "sink or swim", without training in lecturing skills.

Specific complaints centred on the lack of availability of lecturers due to research, consultancy or other commitments, boring and unimaginative delivery of lectures, poor attendance records and punctuality, and inconsistency over deadlines for assignments.

I would change some of the lecturers but I would recommend it. (C)

Some teachers have their own methods which can make it difficult! (C)

I am quite satisfied. To improve it I would fire some of the lecturers. (U)

The lectures are two hours full of waffle. I would prefer more time to do assignments. (C)

It is the best Law course in the country apart from the normal thing of some lecturers who make interesting subjects really boring. (U)

I am satisfied but wish lecturers were more punctual. (U)

It is excellent but I hate the Maths. It is taught in a bad way. The engineers spend three days in an Engineering company each week and then come in and teach. The Maths lecturers are either deaf or idiots. They never listen to us—it is not interesting to engineers. It is one of the best courses in the country and the employers know it. (U)

The lecturers are good and some are famous. (U)

It's pretty good but the lecturers could benefit from some Teacher Training! (U)

The HND is good but the industrial relations lectures were terrible. The lecturer turned up when he wanted. He was the most disgusting man you could ever meet. It sounded a brilliant option in the prospectus. (P)

I would make it stricter. Some people work, some don't. The lecturers have then turned round and said the assignments can be handed in when we liked. People get extensions for the silliest of reasons and then get better marks. It is really unfair—why bother! (P)

Class Sizes

These appear to be growing and students felt that some were now too large. Classes of 150 were not that uncommon, particularly where students from several courses came together for a common module.

We need smaller lectures. All of the faculty share some—180 people is too big. (U)

Organisation

Business departments were the most frequently criticised (perhaps their students expect high standards of management). Rooms being double booked, equipment not working, lectures cancelled without reason, timetables with lectures too thinly spread were all mentioned on a number of occasions.

You have nothing to do, then you get far too much. Not co-ordinated. (C)

Some courses weren't well-planned last year—but I would still recommend it. (C)

Better communication so that the workload can be planned. (C)

They do try hard to integrate it all but it's a bit of a mess. They don't know which rooms are free and stuff like that. I would recommend it. (P)

I love my course it is really well-organised. The College should listen to BTEC more. It just annoys me why people see it (HND) as second-rate. If you actually want to learn something this is the one to do. (P)

I like the practical approach. We are prepared for a job and improve our social skills. (P)

I would recommend it. The organisation of the business course isn't what it should be—they can't even manage themselves. (P)

The course is very interesting but the organisation is disgusting. You hear one thing and the opposite happens. (P)

Lack of Resources

Restricted access to equipment and not enough books (particularly when courses are brought together in very large groups for common subjects) are cited regularly by college and polytechnic students.

We need more books and equipment but I would recommend it. (C)

There aren't enough books to go round. We can't afford to keep paying for photocopying. (P)

Miscellaneous

I would totally NOT recommend the course. (C)

I don't like the course but I would recommend it because you get a degree. (C)

I am doing secondary BEd and most of it is useless—not practical in schools at all. (C)

It is hard. I don't understand all of it. (C)

It's a good course...but it's all new to me! (P)

They expect too high a level on the main subject when you come here. A foundation would be better. (BEd—C)

I am satisfied but I am sure that I could find better! (C)

Not at all—you don't seem to learn anything. (C)

I love my course—you can do practically anything you want in the Arts faculty. (U)

They need better communications between the colleges. (C)

Some lessons you don't learn anything. Sometimes no-one takes any interest. I would recommend it despite that. But I don't feel it's enough—I want to get on. (C)

I am NOT satisfied but I would recommend it. It is the best course in the country from what I know. (U)

I like my course but I would not recommend it to anyone at the moment. They are having great problems finding placements. You start fretting just before exam times. I had to find mine myself. (U)

According to the tutors my course is the best in Europe. (U)

Finally in this chapter we asked the students whether they felt that they had made the right choice of course. Not surprisingly, the majority confirmed that they had (78%). Polytechnic students appeared to be the most assertive (81%). It is again important to stress that these are the views of students who have completed one full year of their course. That so many are still uncertain after twelve months is however very disturbing. The majority of "dropouts" will have left or changed course within the first year and are not shown in these figures. The level of uncertainty is probably higher than the 22% as some students are likely to be "positive" when answering this question.

Table 35   Have you made the right choice of course?

	All%	P%	U%	C%
Yes	78	81	76	78
Uncertain	18	17	19	18
No	4	2	5	4

Chapter 6   Student Expectations

6.1   Introduction

This chapter assesses how confident students are in terms of passing their courses, gaining good honours classifications and gaining suitable employment. We also tested their commitment to particular career paths.

6.2   Academic Confidence

On a scale of 1—10, most second-year students are quite rightly confident of passing their course—the average score being 7.75 (**Table 36**). Barring unforeseen problems, most students who successfully pass their first-year will complete their degree or HND.

Stereotypes are reinforced by these results which indicate that university students are marginally more academically confident (over-confident?) than their peers in polytechnics and colleges. Given their successes at A-level, BTEC, or in entrance examinations, perhaps they are justly more confident. University undergraduates are also more confident about gaining a good honours classification with well over half expecting (aiming for?) a 2(i) or better. On past results a good number are likely to be disappointed! The 20% non-response rate in column two suggests that polytechnic degree students are perhaps either ill-informed about degree classifications or less status conscious.

Table 36   How confident are you of passing your course?

Average rating on scale 1—10 (10 = excellent)

Institution	Rating
All	7.75
Polytechnic	7.78
University	7.93
College	7.56

Table 37   What degree classification do you expect to gain? (Honours students only)

	All%	P%	U%	C%
First	5	5	6	4
2(i)	46	38	57	40
2(ii)	40	33	33	50
Third	4	3	3	6
Pass	1	1	1	2
No response	4	20	0	8

6.3   Future Employment

University undergraduates were again the most confident when it came to assessing their employment prospects, estimating that they had over a 71% chance of gaining suitable employment within three months of graduating. Polytechnic students are also confident although they may be aiming their sights slightly lower when defining "suitable employment". First destination statistics support the case that polytechnic students get jobs just as quickly as university students, although the latter are much more likely to enter post-graduate study.

Table 38   How do you rate your chances of gaining suitable employ ment within three months of graduation?

Average rating on scale 1—10 (10 = excellent)

All	P	U	C
6.94	7.11	7.15	6.61

The final question attempted to measure whether the 1989 intake were likely to pursue a career related to their current course. This will be of particular interest to those professions which are trying to encourage school-leavers into their ranks. **Table 39**'s data show that most students do intend to follow a career related to their course. This is particularly so in the polytechnics and colleges where of the 80% who are likely to do so, 44% and 47% respectively were definite in their assessment.

The relatively low figure for the universities is likely to reflect the less vocational nature of their courses. This is supported by the figures in **Table 39(a)** which show that Humanities students (well represented in the universities) are, naturally, less likely to follow a career directly related to their course for the simple reason that in many cases there is not one to follow! That is not to say that they will not use the knowledge/skills that they will have acquired. Earlier we noted that polytechnic students were more motivated to enter higher education for career progression than were university students.

Table 39 Do you intend to follow a career related to your course/ subject of study?

	All%	P%	U%	C%
Yes definitely	39	44	27	47
Yes probably	34 }73	36 }80	33 }60	33 }80
Uncertain	18	13	24	14
Unlikely	5	4	10	3
No	4	3	6	3

That BEd students are the most likely to follow a related profession was expected: most students have entered the course because they want to become teachers and all will have been interviewed to ensure that they are serious and have the correct aptitude.

Vocational subject areas such Engineering/Technology, the Built Environment and Science did not fare too well. Has the campaign to generate more technically-based students merely succeeded in attracting marginal students whose long-term commitment is not too strong? Engineering students were, remember, the least likely to recommend their course (**Table 33a**).

Table 39(a) Do you intend to follow a career related to your course/ subject of study?

Subject Area	"Yes" %
Education/Teacher Training	89
IT/Computing	85
Art/Design/Music/Drama	84
Health/Social Services	83
Business/Law	82
Engineering/Technology	77
Science/Mathematics	60
Built Environment	58
Humanities/Social Science	55

Chapter 7   Aspects of Student Life

7.1   Introduction

In this chapter we examine four related aspects of student life, namely: accommodation, finances, student social life and student problems. The aim is to give careers advisers and applicants some hard data which may, or may not, support their hunches about where students live, how many feel homesick and the proportion of students who have overdrafts.

7.2   Student Accommodation

In what type of accommodation do students start their undergraduate existence? The answer for the majority (58%) is the traditional hall of residence managed by the institution. A flat or house shared with other young people (usually students) was second (14%) followed by parental home (9%) and "other" (8%). This latter category was made up mostly of mature students living in their own home.

If we examine the figures more closely they reveal remarkable differences between the three sectors. The great majority of university students start out in halls (81%) as do college students, although to a much lesser degree (54%). By contrast, only 29% of polytechnic students start in halls—fewer than live in privately rented houses/flats. These figures illustrate the relative lack of accommodation under the control of the polytechnics: most of their students live in the community whilst most university students live "on-campus". These contrasting life-styles are likely to have an impact on the relationship between the student and his/her institution. It may explain why polytechnic alumni associations have not been as successful as their university counterparts. Polytechnic students tend to have a closer relationship with their course than with their institution as a whole (as suggested by earlier results). The more middle class nature of the university student body, the family history of higher education, and the greater numbers from private/grammar schools which inculcate the "club" mentality may also have an impact.

Table 40 Type of accommodation used by first-year students

	All%	P%	U%	C%
Halls	58	29	81	54
Flat/house	14	30	5	12
Parental home	9	10	3	14
Other	8	11	6	9
Lodgings	7	13	3	6
Bed-sit	2	4	1	2
Hostel	1	1	0	3
No response	1	2	1	0

It is not only the type of accommodation that is of interest to freshers: availability and quality are of the utmost importance. We asked students to rate the ease with which they found suitable accommodation for the start of their course **(Table 41)**. The figures in the left hand column reflect the findings in **Table 40**, with the vast majority of university students believing the process of obtaining suitable accommodation to be very easy, the score of 9.08 reflecting the fact that most obtained places in halls. The overall figures for the colleges and polytechnics were much lower as a greater proportion had to find private rented accommodation.

The second column eliminates the impact of the halls of residence factor and reveals a much more even distribution of responses. This provides some evidence to suggest that the level of assistance provided by the institutions to new students seeking private sector accommodation is generally similar in each sector. The colleges of higher education rating of 5.09 is relatively low. This is probably due to the more rural/isolated location of a large number of the colleges. In such locations the availability of private rented accommodation will be more limited.

What these figures do illustrate is that those students who are not allocated places in halls have considerably greater difficulty in securing suitable accommodation. The availability of college accommodation is certainly an important part of the marketing mix when recruiting students. Heist research with potential applicants has revealed that accommodation information is of vital importance: most sixth-formers ask that more information should be included in prospectuses. A recent analysis of PCAS applications by Heist showed a positive correlation between availability of college accommodation (as a proportion of enrolments) and the number of applications per admission. In this particular survey the students ranked accommodation the ninth most important factor when shortlisting institutions.

Table 41   How difficult was it to find suitable accommodation?

Average rating on scale 1—10 (10 = very easy)

	All Students	Private Rented Sector Only
All	8.25	5.26
Polytechnic	6.50	5.19
University	9.08	5.77
College	8.57	5.09

In terms of the quality of the accommodation we decided to measure only one aspect—a feature that could be easily quantified: distance from usual place of study (**Table 42**). The figures again reflect the university sector's ability to accommodate their first-year students in halls—the majority of which are on, or very close to, the campus/teaching facilities. Polytechnic students have the greatest average distance to travel to study which is an additional financial burden. This is in addition to the likely higher rents which they pay compared with those in college halls. In addition to the relative availability of halls, these figures also reflect the greater local/mature profile of the polytechnic and college sectors. Those travelling in excess of six miles to study are, in the main, mature students living in their own homes or local students commuting from their parental home.

Table 42   How many miles from accommodation to main place of study?

Miles	0	1	2	3	4	5	6/more	Average (miles)
All %	44	15	11	7	3	4	16	2.66
Polytechnic %	21	20	16	13	5	5	20	3.66
University %	58	14	9	6	3	3	7	1.70
College %	45	13	10	5	3	3	21	2.87

Note: Average based on 6/more being given a value of 6. The actual average is therefore higher than the figure shown.

7.3 Student Finances

With the freezing of student grants, the introduction of student loans and the radical changes to the benefit system vis-à-vis student claimants, the whole issue of student finance is once again centre-stage.

The survey revealed that 52% of all students were in the red at the end of their first year, with polytechnic students the most likely to be overdrawn at the bank (54%). The students in the focus groups complained about lack of financial/budgetary skills and many argued that such life skills should be part of the sixth/fifth-form curriculum and that financial counselling for freshers should be more widely available from the college in association with the banks and the students' unions. Some students complained that the advisers in the banks were not graduates and therefore were not sympathetic to their particular problems.

These figures relate to the academic year ending 1990—before the introduction of the loans system the freezing of grants and the withdrawal of state benefits. With the real value of the grant being eroded by inflation and the availability of easy credit, it is likely that the spread and depth of student indebtedness will have risen over the past year.

Table 43 Proportion of students with an overdraft at the end of their first year

	All%	P%	U%	C%
Yes	52	54	50	52
No	48	46	50	48

Of those in the red the average overdraft was approximately £292 (polytechnic); £270 (college) and £259 (university). 25% of all students were £250 or more in the red at the end of the first year.

The financial plight of students tends to be cumulative: these figures only reflect the first year. From the second year the great majority will live in private accommodation (as opposed to halls) which is usually considerably more expensive and likely to be further from the place of study (thereby leading to higher transport costs). Many students have relied on summer vacation work to stabilise or reduce their overdraft levels. In times of recession the availability of such work tends to reduce sharply.

Table 44 provides further evidence about the social class of students in the three sectors. Far more polytechnic and college student receive the full grant than do university students. **Table 45** shows that whilst the majority of those not on full grants enjoy full parental contributions there are a considerable number (24%) who do not.

To put these results into better perspective 16% of all students do not receive a full grant or full parental contributions. Such students are clearly disadvantaged. Broken down, the results indicate that college (19%) and polytechnic (15%) students are more likely to be in this position than those in the universities (13%). Whether this is due to the parents being unable or unwilling to pay, or the student not claiming the contribution due to relationship problems we do not know.

Table 44   Students receiving the full LEA maintenance grant

	Yes %	No %
All	35	65
Polytechnic	39	61
University	7	73
College	42	58

Table 45   Percentage of students NOT receiving full LEA grant who obtained full parental contributions

	%
All	76
Polytechnic	75
University	82
College	69

Almost a quarter of all students appear to be working during term-time to supplement their grants as reported in **Table 46**. As we have already shown, university students appear to have more healthy finances— consistent with this result (we hypothesise that students work out of necessity) is the finding that far fewer of them work during term (12%) compared with college (30%) or polytechnic (28%) students.

Bar work appears to be the most popular work, with a well-known chain of hamburger restaurants providing a great number of employment opportunities. Few students gained work related to their studies and most was of the unskilled variety.

Of students who did work, the great majority were employed for between seven and twenty hours a week. Polytechnic and college students worked longer hours than their university peers with 84% (polytechnic) and 77% (college) students working more than seven hours compared with only 70% of university students.

Table 46   Proportion of students having a job during term-time in first year

	All%	P%	U%	C%
Most of time	12	15	5	17
Intermittently	11	13	7	13
No	76	71	87	70
No response	1	1	1	0

Most of time / Intermittently combined: }23 }28 }12 }30

University students seem to benefit from a wider range of sources of income than do polytechnic or college students (**Table 47**). They benefit more from vacation employment, sponsorship and investment income. College and polytechnic students rely more on term-time wages and social security. With the latter being cut back, it is college and polytechnic students who can be expected to suffer most as a consequence.

Table 47   Sources of student income other than grants/parental contributions

	All%	P%	U%	C%
Social security	8	14	8	33
Wages (term)	17	21	10	22
Investment	5	5	6	3
Sponsorship	4	3	7	1
Wages (holidays)	51	50	56	47
Other	9	8	9	10

These financial results are rather disturbing. It would appear that more students are being forced into "working through college" as a result of financial difficulties. This is particularly so in the college/ polytechnic sectors which have been at the forefront of widening access both in terms of age and class. Is the likelihood of debt an attraction for the prospective student? Debt of a short-term and relatively minor nature is unlikely to deter the majority of university applicants who appear from our results to be more confident individuals for whom higher education is a natural state. They also appear to have a more sound financial platform. Polytechnic and college students, however, appear to be less confident and less affluent. The thought of debt may well be less palatable to these applicants, their parents and partners.

7.4 Student Social life

To many on the outside, including potential applicants, student life is often thought to revolve around the various clubs and societies. In all, 69% of our sample had been a member of a society in the first year. However, there were significant variations between the three sectors, as the results in **Table 48** illustrate. Do these figures reflect the relative paucity of clubs at polytechnics and colleges or do they reflect the nature of the student attending the institutions or the greater distances most have to travel from their accommodation to their institution? If we refer back to **Table 32** we find that the students in polytechnics and colleges rated sporting facilities, social clubs and the students' unions (usually the organisers of societies, etc) lower than their university peers. In **Table 29** the college students had rated poor facilities as the second worst feature of their institution. These results tend to support the first hypothesis. The fact that far more students live on campus at universities **(Table 40)** in the first year is also likely to be a significant factor explaining the 87% participation rate at such institutions.

Table 48   Were you a member of a club or society in the first year?

	Yes %	No %
All	69	31
Polytechnic	62	38
University	87	13
College	54	46

According to the findings presented in **Table 49**, students return home once a term on average, with college students returning more frequently (every seven weeks on average) than polytechnic students (eight weeks) or university students (ten weeks).

There is a strong positive correlation between distance from home and the frequency of return visits. There are two obvious explanations: students choosing to study furthest from home do so because they have little desire to visit their relatives on a regular basis (the obverse being true for more local students); alternatively, the relative scarcity of return journeys made by distant students is simply the product of costs in terms of fares and time. What evidence we have tends to support the former explanation because so many students (29%) placed "distance from home" as an important criterion when short-listing where to apply (**Table 22**). Further evidence is supplied by those studying over 160 miles from home, 12% of whom claim never to have returned home since starting college—a result which cannot be explained away by reference to the cost of rail fares!

Table 49   Distance from home and frequency of return journeys

Distance (Miles)	Frequency (Weeks)
0-19	3.1
20-39	3.4
40-59	4.4
60-79	4.8
80-99	5.3
100-119	5.8
120-139	5.9
140-159	6.5
160+	6.0*

* (12% of those in this category claimed never to return home)

The stereotype student is usually one who is having a good time and making new friends, but is this really the case? It is often claimed that the lonely are most likely to be surrounded by large numbers of people. Nowhere fits this description better than a campus.

Our results in **Table 50** suggest that most students find it no more difficult to make friends at college than they had expected before entering higher education. Indeed, far more (34%) claimed that it had been easier than those who said that it was more difficult (12%). College students were the least likely to find making friends more difficult than anticipated, thereby supporting the "small and friendly" description often used by such institutions in their promotional materials.

Table 50   Making friends in the first year

	All%	P%	U%	C%
More difficult than expected	12	15	12	11
Less difficult than expected	34	35	35	33
As expected	54	50	53	56

We have found a correlation between the answers in **Table 50** and whether respondents had resided in halls of residence. Those who had been in halls were much more likely to claim that making friends had been easier than expected than were those who were not in halls. They were also less likely to claim that making friends had been more difficult than those in other (less social) forms of accommodation.

7.5   Student Problems

The final question in our survey examined what were loosely termed student problems. The questionnaire included the list of the problems as outlined in **Table 51** and the students were asked to tick the three which they believed were most often encountered by fellow students. We did not ask the blunt question "which of these problems have you suffered from?" because we felt that a question phrased in the third person would be more likely to generate valid results. The list of conditions was based on a survey which identified the most common issues that student counsellors were confronted with over a one-year period. Not all of the categories are mutually exclusive because in many cases the record of consultation had not been explicit.

Top of the list came finances with 71%. This is much higher than the 52% who are in the red (**Table 43**). However, we should not equate financial problems with being overdrawn. The problem may be that students would "like more money" rather than the fact that they have none at all. Consistent with other results, fewer university students felt that finance was a problem than did polytechnic and college respondents.

Other results also appear to be consistent with earlier findings. University students scored homesickness relatively low, confirming the view of the focus groups that those from boarding/private schools had learned to be more independent. However, relationship problems were relatively high, perhaps reflecting the problems created by single-sex schools?

95

44% of university students chose examination anxiety as a common problem. This relatively high score may reflect the pressure that university students experience from parents and peers to "succeed". Universities also tend to rely more heavily on examinations compared with polytechnics/colleges where some continual assessment is the norm.

Housing was a relatively small issue for university students compared with those in polytechnics where it was rated second.

The much vaunted drugs issue hardly surfaced at all with only 2% believing it to be an important problem for first-year students. This may be because those who take drugs do so relatively privately (unless it gets out-of-hand) and fellow students may not be aware of the problem. Students may also consider the taking of some of the more minor drugs not to be a problem.

Table 51   What problems do students encounter in their first year?

All mentions from multiple choice

	All%	P%	U%	C%
Financial	71	76	65	75
Examination anxiety	41	37	44	38
Lack of confidence	37	36	37	39
Depressed	34	28	36	36
Relationships	30	24	37	28
Career/course indecision	27	26	28	27
Anxiety	26	21	28	28
Homesickness	24	25	20	27
Housing	22	38	14	20
Loneliness	17	16	20	16
Alcohol	10	7	13	9
Parents	6	6	5	9
Sex	4	3	4	4
Drugs	2	3	2	2

Comments from the Focus Groups

The groups were asked "what problems did you encounter in the first year at college?" The following selection of quotes illustrate the main issues raised. There was considerable and consistent criticism of the personal tutoring system. Where it did work, the student gained a friend and an essential crutch during the difficult first few months. This, sadly, was the exception. Most comments about personal tutors were very negative—they were apparently never available, were not sympathetic or practical in their advice, etc. Most gave the impression that it was a part of the job that they would rather not do. One can sympathise: dealing with student personal problems is not easy—even for the well-intentioned amateur.

Those who had been to professional counsellors were more positive but there was clear resistance to using the service: some felt it was an admission of failure; others claimed that the counsellors were remote and were people that they rarely saw. "I couldn't discuss a personal problem with someone I had never met before!" was how one female student summed it up. Many second-year students were still not sure if a counselling service actually existed in their institution. In-house counsellors should promote their services more effectively and in a more personal and face-to-face way.

Dealing with problems

If anyone in hall has a problem I think there is a camaraderie and you can't but help noticing if someone is down. Friends tend to help out. (P)

I was very fortunate to get into halls—a real blessing. There is always someone's door to knock on. (P)

There are people to help with problems but I would not talk to them about a personal problem. (U)

My personal adviser wasn't interested at all. (U)

There was no-one I could pop in and see. My personal tutor did nothing whatsoever to help. (U)

I was assigned a personal tutor who wasn't any use at all. (U)

Making Friends

I had been with the same friends from the age of five. I had forgotten how to make new friends. (P)

I was a bit homesick. Separation from special people rather than loneliness. (P)

In my first term I was shy, no friends, homesick and wanted to leave. Tell people to stick it out—you will get settled in. (U)

The social life is centred around drinking. If you don't drink, making friends can be more difficult. (P)

Smile at people. So many people don't. People like happy people. (U)

If you are not in halls you only meet people on your course. (C)

I was homesick. I wouldn't want to go through being a fresher again. (C)

It's easy to make friends as long as you make the effort. (C)

Finances

When I got my grant cheque I went totally mad. Going to the disco not on books! (P)

Handling banks and insurance companies. They sort themselves out in the end! (P)

Finances are the big problem. Students go out and spend madly in the first few weeks. Then they realise that it's gone. They go to the bank and ask for more. Most don't know where it's gone. (P)

My grant came really late—it was a crisis! (U)

Course-related

I think adapting to the new way of life. I found it difficult to concentrate on the work. (P)

I could not get motivated until the work deadlines had actually gone. Lecturers are far too ready to give extensions for work. (U)

Our course is small so we get together and winge. It helps. (U)

You don't get much one-to-one. Lecturers are keen to do as little as possible. (U)

Too many people worry about the work instead of actually doing any. (U)

I had a major crisis on the first day—I panicked, but the College was so supportive and I got through it. (C)

The work came all at once—not spread out or managed. (C)

Trying to remember everyone's name was a problem. (P)

I shared a room with a girl. We hated each other totally. (U)

Be honest when filling in the accommodation form. You might end up sharing with someone with whom you have nothing in common. (U)

Love at first sight was wonderful. Then she went out with someone else on the course and I had a really bad second term. Don't fall in love on the first day as it restricts your chance to make lots of friends. (U)

There have been a lot of muggings and rapes. It is not safe here. (U)

I was the first person in my family to come to university. I had no-one to ask what to expect. (U)

The first problem was that the landlord had a heart attack on the first night and the landlady took to the bottle. She treated us like her daughters—death at dawn if the kitchen was a mess. We stuck it for two months. (C)

Lots of people in the house got into stupid little arguments—it got to horrific levels. (C)

Chapter 8 Key Findings: Mature vs Traditional Students

8.1 Introduction

The questionnaire survey was designed for traditional students those who entered higher education from sixth-form or FE college. However, due to the inability of many institutions to be able to discriminate between mature and traditional students for the purposes of distributing the questionnaire, 484 completed forms were returned from mature students—those aged 21 and over at the point of entry on to their course. As a result, we are able to compare responses from these two groups and provide a valuable insight into how the decision-making and opinions of mature and traditional students differ. We have focused on certain key findings where clear differences were identified.

8.2 Location

Mature students are significantly more likely to attend a local higher education institution than are traditional students. 43.8% of the mature students were studying at an institution less than 39 miles from home compared with only 18.7% of the traditional age group. However, mature students are not confined to local colleges: 25% were 160 miles or more from home, compared with 32.6% of school-leavers.

The mature student is more likely to be an urban dweller. Approximately 52% of mature respondents had been living in a major town or city when they applied compared with only 40% of the traditional age group. This may help to explain why institutions located in major conurbations tend to attract a greater proportion of mature students.

8.3 Decision Timing

Conventional wisdom suggests that many mature entrants to higher education are people who slipped through the net at 18, that is to say, people who intended to continue their education but who, for academic, social or economic reasons, did not enter higher education when they left school. The results of this survey do not support that hypothesis. 70% of the mature students said that they did not firmly decide on higher education until they were aged at least 20.

When it came to the choice of subject in higher education their decision-making was later still, with almost 82% confirming that they chose their current subject of study after the age of 20.

8.4 Advisers and Influencers

It was a real surprise to learn that the mature students were much more likely to have an immediate relative or close friend with a degree in their subject of study or who was employed in a related profession. A significant 47% had such a friend/relative compared with 37% of the traditional students. Of those with such a contact, 76% of mature students had discussed their plans with them (84% for traditional students).

Far fewer mature students (24%) had a parent with a degree than had traditional students (42%). This was to be expected because the parent of a mature student is likely to be in his or her mid to late forties or older. Only a very small proportion of this age group would be likely to have a degree. That 24% of mature students have such a parent is actually a very high figure.

55% of the mature students questioned had not sought any formal careers/education guidance before entering their course compared with only 20% of school-leavers. Of those who had taken advice the dominant counsellors had been LEA careers officers (43%), careers teachers (FE college—20%) and subject teachers for previous courses (22%). Overall, the mature students rated the advice given much more highly than did school-leavers, with over half rating the advice as good or excellent.

Mature students were more likely to be recommended to apply to a specific institution (29%) than were school-leavers (21%). The reason is that, in many cases, the student is directed to the nearest college because of the importance of travel-to-study factor. It is fair to assume that careers advisers are better able to give advice about local institutions and would therefore feel more confident about offering direct recommendations in such circumstances.

Where the mature student had been given advice about the best type of institution for them to apply to, polytechnics were the most often recommended (32%).

8.5   Short-listing Institutions

Mature students appear to use the same criteria as traditional applicants when short-listing where to apply. However, the weight given to the various criteria is, as expected, significantly different, as **Table 52** shows.

Table 52   Criteria for short-listing institutions: mature vs traditional students

All mentions to open question.

Top five answers

	Mature %	Traditional %
The course	52	65
Distance from home	44	26
Town/city	39	55
Recommended/reputation	27	30
Entry requirements	12	16

Two significant differences emerge. Mature students are much more concerned about distance from home, whereas traditional students give greater consideration to the nature of the town/city in which the institution is based. It was very surprising to note that entry qualifications played such a minor role for mature students. Unlike the position for traditional applicants, where different courses have varying "price tags" in the form of entry grades, mature students are usually faced with a situation where they will be accepted without formal qualifications. In such circumstances the price is consistent to most courses.

8.6   Induction and Familiarisation

Most course admissions tutors are keen to interview mature applicants to ensure that they have the aptitude and skills to succeed. This policy is evidenced in our figures which show that the matures were much more likely to have attended an interview/open day for their course than school leavers (77% against 64%). Matures were also much more likely to be attending their first choice college (78% against 62%) due, no doubt, to more liberal admissions policies.

103

The nature and content of the interview was very similar for mature students except that they were much less likely to have visited the students' union facilities. Overall, mature students were slightly less happy with the induction procedures for new students than their more youthful counterparts, giving an average rating of 5.9 against 6.2 on a scale of 1—10.

8.7   Opinions of the College

Mature students are consistently less satisfied with their college than are school-leavers. 87% of matures would recommend the college (compared with 88% for young entrants) but the strength of the recommendation is far less solid, in that most had some reservations.

When asked to rate aspects of their college the following results emerged:

Table 53   Rating of aspects of the institution: mature vs traditional students

Average rating on scale 1—10 (10 = excellent)

	Mature	Traditional
Students' union	5.4	5.3
Sports facilities	5.9	6.1
Bars/catering	5.2	5.8
Entertainment	4.9	5.5
Social clubs	5.4	6.0
Library/learning	6.8	7.1
Private study facilities	5.3	5.9
Computer/IT support	5.8	6.4
Overall average	5.6	6.0

With the exception of the students' union, mature students rated the institution lower on all aspects, but particularly the social facilities, clubs, bars and entertainment.

With regard to the worst aspect of the institution, there was little difference between the mature and traditional students with "poor organisation" attracting the most votes in both cases. However, there was some divergence of opinion when it came to identifying the best aspect of the college. Both mature (21%) and traditional (27%) placed "atmosphere" top, but mature students gave much more emphasis to the quality of staff (17%) and staff-student relations (13%) than did younger students who appeared to be more concerned with college social life (10%).

8.8   Opinions of Courses

A slightly higher proportion of mature students would recommend their course (88.6% against 87.5%) and the strength of that recommendation would be stronger, with over half having no reservations at all.

This strong support for the course is echoed in the results relating to specific aspects of course delivery (**Table 54**) where in most cases the mature students rated the course higher than their school-leaver colleagues.

Table 54   Specific aspects of course delivery: mature vs traditional students

Average rating on scale 1—10 (10 = excellent)

	Mature	Traditional
Organisation/efficiency	5.8	5.9
Quality of lecturing	7.0	6.6
Resources/equipment	6.1	6.4
Subject content	7.5	7.2
Personal support	6.9	6.4
Communication with staff	7.2	6.6
Student participation in course development	6.5	6.2
Average	7.0	6.6
Overall learning experience	7.5	7.2

The mature students rate communication with staff, student participation and personal support more highly than do traditional students—perhaps because these aspects are more important to them. Mature students also rate the lecturing quality more positively.

Mature students are more likely to find the volume of work related to their course higher than they anticipated than is the case for school-leavers. 37% said that the volume was higher than expected compared with only 15% who though it was less. Mature students, out of practice in the art of learning, are likely to find the first year of higher education more time-consuming than traditional students with more recent study experience.

8.9   Student Confidence

The stereo-type mature student is often considered to be less confident than the successful school-leaver who is well versed in learning techniques. So much for the theory. In our sample, the mature students were considerably more confident and sure of their future plans.

The matures had an 80% rating when asked about their level of confidence about passing the course, compared with 77% for the traditional age range. Over 60% of the over 21s felt they would gain a 2(i) or better compared with only 53% of younger students.

A greater proportion of mature students said that they were likely to follow a career related to their course (80%) than were their younger peers (70%) and the over 21s were also more bullish about their job prospects—rating their chances of obtaining suitable employment within three months of graduating at 76% compared with only 68% for younger undergraduates.

Finances

67% of the mature respondents were receiving a full LEA grant compared with only 29% of the school-leaver age group but mature students were just as likely to be in the red at the end of the first year as their school-leaver colleagues. The mature student is likely to have a larger overdraft than the younger entrant averaging £378. Mature students have had longer in which to accumulate a debt and are likely to have a greater number of financial commitments.

Student Life

As would be expected, mature students are much less likely to be a member of a club or society (51% against 72%). The older student is likely to have more family commitments and friends in the wider community. As many also commute to study, evening activities are also more difficult to attend with any regularity.

Chapter 9   Key Results by Gender

9.1   Introduction

We have analysed the results by gender to identify any differences in the responses given by male and female students. Some old chestnuts appear to be laid to rest—female students are no more likely to study locally to be close to mother's knee than are male students. However, many stereo-types are reinforced: males appear to be more confident and more concerned with academic values than are female students. This chapter contains edited highlights: the complete set of statistics would fill another report!

9.2   Subjects of Study

The gender balance of the various subject areas in higher education is a matter of public record. Clearing house statistics provide a complete and accurate picture. Our sample appears to be typical in that males dominate in Engineering and Technology, Built Environment, Science and Maths, IT and Computing and, to a lesser extent, Medicine. Females are in the majority in subject areas such as Art/Drama/Music/Design, Health and Social Services, Humanities, Business and Law, and, especially, Teacher Training.

9.3   Location

Females were only marginally more likely to be studying locally than were males and a higher proportion of females were studying over 160 miles from home (31%) than males (23.8%). If a graph plotting distance from home is created, the path of the curves for males and females are almost identical.

9.4   Decision Timing

There is a clear difference between the sexes with respect to the timing of their key decisions concerning higher education: girls make their decisions much earlier in their school life than do boys. In terms of firmly deciding to aim for a place in higher education, girls are, on average, about a year ahead of boys. Over 66% of females had decided to go on to higher education before entering the sixth-form compared

107

with only 59% of males. This result is supported by the finding that showed more males had seriously considered a job whilst in the sixth-form than had females (30% against 25%).

Female students also appear to choose their subject of study slightly earlier. 30% of females had decided on their subject of study before entering the sixth-form (which no doubt influenced their choice of A-levels and BTECs) compared with 26% of males. Within the sixth-form years, the upper sixth is also more important to males than females in terms of subject choice—again confirming the later nature of the male decision. Those trying to persuade females to consider Engineering or Sciences therefore have to start communicating with their audience early in their schooling.

9.5   Advisers and Influencers

There was little difference between the sexes in terms of whether or not they had a close friend or immediate relative with some experience of their current subject area. However, where such a person or persons existed, girls were more likely to have asked their advice (85% compared with 79% for boys). In such cases, females were also more likely to have been given advice about which specific institutions to which they should apply. By relating this answer to a number of other results, we suggest that the differences shown here are connected to the fact that more females have friends/relatives involved in the creative subject areas and teaching. Within these niche markets a number of colleges have been able to develop reputations and it is within these areas that recommendation is more likely to take place. For example, although similar proportions of males and females had a parent with a degree or equivalent, more females had a parent who had been to Teacher Training college or a specialist college (such as Art and Design, Music, etc.) than had males.

A slightly greater proportion of females took advice about higher education from an LEA adviser or a teacher than did males and generally they were more satisfied with the advice given. The majority of female students had taken advice from at least two different types of adviser with LEA adviser and careers teacher being the most important. At least half of the males who took advice also spoke to more than one adviser but in their cases the careers teacher in school was the leading choice. Subject teachers appear to be marginally more important for females than males.

Once again, females were more likely to have been recommended a specific institution to which they should apply (23%). Where a specific type of institution was suggested by the careers adviser/teacher a higher proportion of females to males were encouraged to apply to specialist colleges, colleges of higher education and polytechnics. The proportion encouraged to apply to university was virtually identical.

9.6 Short-listing Institutions

Males and females use very similar criteria when choosing institutions and the ranking of those criteria is almost identical. However, there are important differences in terms of the proportion of students mentioning each factor.

Both males and females place the course and related features as the most critical factor. However, it is important to more females than males. 68% of females placed it in their top three compared with 56% of males. The specific town/city in which an institution is located was of equal importance to both sexes, mentioned by 52%.

Distance from home was mentioned by more females (33%) than males (24%). Earlier results suggest that more females are keen to get well away from home rather than to stay local. More males, on the other hand, are concerned about the reputation and status of the institution (34%) than are females (26%).

9.7 Opinions of the Institution

Female students appear to be much less critical/more supportive of their college than are males. For example, more would recommend the institution to a friend (89% against 83%) and they also gave their institution a higher rating for their induction than did males (6.2 rating against 5.9).

Satisfaction rating with various aspects of the institution is shown in **Table 55**. The overall average supports the finding that females are generally more positive/less critical towards their college. It is interesting that females out-rate the males for the students' union, bars/catering, entertainment, sporting facilities, and social clubs/facilities (i.e. the social or non-academic aspects), whereas the males score the library, private study facilities and computer/IT support more highly (i.e. the academic aspects).

109

Table 55   Satisfaction with aspects of the institution by gender

Average rating on scale of 1—10 (10 = excellent)

	Male	Female
Library/learning resources	7.1	6.9
Computer/IT support	6.5	6.1
Sporting facilities	5.8	6.2
Social clubs	5.8	6.0
Private study facilities	5.9	5.8
Bars/catering	5.6	5.8
Entertainment	5.2	5.6
Students' union	5.0	5.6
Average rating	5.9	6.0

When asked about the best and worst aspects of their institution, opinion was divided, although the top ten answers were the same for both sexes. In terms of best things, far more females mentioned "atmosphere" (29%) than males (18%). In terms of frequency of mention, females placed the course second and the environment third whereas the result was reversed for males.

Turning to the worst things, the greatest number of males placed "atmosphere between students" top (9.2%) followed by poor organisation (7.7%). Females were more concerned about poor organisation (11.1% and top) and placed the atmospheric issue second (8.0%).

9.8   Opinions of Courses

A larger proportion of females were likely to recommend their course (89%) than males (85%) and the strength of the recommendation was likely to be stronger as almost half of all females said they would definitely recommend it without reservation.

Table 56 shows how the two sexes differed in their rating of specific aspects of the course. It is remarkable that females rated all aspects higher than males: do females have a lower threshold of satisfaction or do they receive a better service?

When we asked if students believed that they had made the right choice of course, more females (79%) claimed that they had than did males

(75%). Perhaps females are more content with their choices and are therefore more content with the delivery of the course?

Table 56   Rating of specific aspects of the course by gender

Average score on scale 1—10 (10 = excellent)

	Male	**Female**
Organisation	5.8	5.9
Quality of lecturing	6.6	6.8
Resources/equipment	6.3	6.4
Subject content	7.2	7.4
Personal support	6.3	6.6
Communication with staff	6.6	6.8
Student participation in course	5.2	5.8
Average	6.3	6.5
Overall learning experience	7.1	7.4

9.9   Student Confidence

Male students are more confident about passing their course than females (8.1 compared with 7.5 on a scale of 1—10). This difference was exaggerated when they were asked about the class of honours degree that they were likely to achieve. 64% of males said a first or 2(i) compared with only 48% of females.

When it came to employment, the male ego was still riding high: they rated their chances of obtaining suitable employment within three months of graduation at 7.2 out of 10 compared with a more modest 6.7 assessment from the females.

9.10   Finances

In our sample, slightly more males (37%) received a full LEA grant than did females (35%). The proportion who had the grant "made up" by parents was roughly similar. A greater proportion of male students received sponsorship support than did females due to the fact than most sponsored places are in the male-dominated subjects of Science and Engineering. Males and females had an equal propensity to work in term time and during the vacations.

Taking the sources of income into account, it would appear that female students are more prudent with their finances than males: slightly fewer were in the red at the end of their first year (51% against 54%) and the average level of their overdraft was much lower at an estimated £241 against £301.

Where does the male student's money go? More are members of clubs and societies (71% against 66%). Males travel home to visit parents/ friends no more or less often than females, so transport expenditure does not seem to account for the higher spend. Females do seem to be positively discriminated in favour of when college hall places are allocated. As a result a greater proportion of males have to live in private sector rented accommodation where rents are generally much higher. This may explain some of their greater financial problems.

9.11 First-year Problems

There were significant variations in the response to the question "what sort of problems do you rate as most common amongst first-year students?" None of the problem areas was mentioned by more than 32% of males—the top "problem" being "feeling depressed". Second for males was relationships (30%), followed by course indecision (27%), lack of confidence (24%), general anxiety (19%) and homesickness (19%).

The top issue for females appears to be examination anxiety (42%), followed by lack of confidence (41%), feeling depressed (36%), relationships (31%), general anxiety (27%) and homesickness (27%).

Overall these results support the view that male students are more confident (or wish to appear more confident) than their female colleagues.

Chapter 10   Key Results by Sector

10.1   Introduction

This chapter contains no new information but simply a summary of the main results for each sector: polytechnics, universities and colleges of higher education. The findings demonstrate that there are a considerable number of differences between the three sectors in terms of the nature of students, their decision-making, and their opinions.

10.2   Profile

Our sample indicates that the university fresher is more likely to be a male school-leaver than is the case in polytechnics and colleges where females form a higher proportion of entrants and where there are larger numbers of mature students. Students from independent schools are much more likely to be found in universities and former further education students are more likely to enter a college or polytechnic.

Virtually all university students are studying for honours degrees. This is less so in colleges and polytechnics where the HND is available.

10.3   Location

Colleges were much more likely to have a large proportion of local students compared with universities whose students appear to be much more likely to choose institutions some distance from home.

A greater proportion of college students (60%) come from rural areas than is the case in the universities (57%) and the polytechnics (53%). There may be a correlation between this result and the more small/rural nature of many of the colleges.

10.4   Choices in Schools

University students seem to make their choices earlier than others, both in terms of aiming for higher education and choice of higher education subject. Fewer university students seriously considered employment whilst at school—higher education appears to be the natural climax to their education. Polytechnic and college students choose their subjects later and the decision was more related to career prospects.

10.5 Advisers

University students were the most likely to have taken advice from a teacher or careers adviser. Form tutors and subject teachers are more important sources of information and advice for them than is the case for their colleagues in colleges and polytechnics where the careers adviser and careers teacher dominate the advice stakes.

College students were the most likely to have been advised to apply to a named institution (26%). This is probably due to the more specialist nature of college provision. University students were the most likely to have been advised to go to a particular type of institution (60%). Of those who received such advice all had been directed towards university.

86% of polytechnic students had been advised to apply to that type of institution but only 47% of college students had been pointed in the direction of that sector. This suggests that more college students are not attending their preferred institution.

Polytechnic, and particularly college, students are more likely to have a friend or relative with experience of their chosen subject of study. This is likely to be the result of the more vocational nature of these two sectors' provision. College students with such contacts were the most likely to discuss their plans with them (82%). The friends/relatives of college students were also more likely to recommend a named institution (35%).

We have noted that for most university students higher education was the natural choice. Far more university students have at least one parent (47%) with a degree or similar than do polytechnic or college students. There appears to be a clear link here.

41% of university students have a parent with a university degree compared with only 4% of polytechnic students with a polytechnic degree-holding parent and 27% of college students with a college graduate as a parent. Polytechnics have obviously had a shorter life and therefore have far fewer alumni who are parents of teenagers. In such circumstances it is little wonder that the majority of parents discriminate in favour of universities against the other two alternatives.

10.6 Criteria for Short-listing Institutions

Distance from home was cited more frequently by college and polytechnic students as were academic facilities. More university students mentioned the course, the host city/town, reputation and first impressions.

10.7 Transition to Higher Education

Far fewer polytechnic students had been for an open day or interview at their present institution than had college or university students. This profile suggests that a large proportion are not at their first-choice institution. College students were the most likely to have had an interview. This may again reflect the nature of the courses in the sector: most creative and all BEd courses insist on interviews, auditions or presentations of work.

Universities were rated slightly higher for their induction procedures at 6.3 compared with 6.0 for the polytechnics and colleges.

10.8 Opinions of the College

The greatest number of polytechnic and college students cited poor organisation as the worst aspect of their institution whereas for university undergraduates it was the bad atmosphere and student mix. This was largely related to cliques, and friction between those from maintained and independent schools.

However, when it came to identifying the best aspects of the institution, atmosphere was also placed top by the largest number of university students. In this context, atmosphere seems to be related to the relaxed life and community spirit on campus. Atmosphere was also rated top by polytechnic students and most especially by college students who liked the intimate and friendly nature that the smaller institution offered.

University students were the most likely to recommend their institution, college students the least likely. All three sectors had high ratings.

University libraries, sports facilities and social clubs were highly rated. The polytechnics scored well for computing/IT support and for private study facilities. College students were consistently the least satisfied with their institution and its facilities, particularly the social clubs available.

10.9 Opinions of Courses

College students were marginally the most likely to recommend their course, which is in direct contrast to their opinions of the college as a whole. University students were the least likely to recommend.

However, satisfaction ratings for the courses were highest in the university sector and lowest for polytechnics, although the overall results were very similar. Polytechnics achieved the top rating for quality of lecturing and student participation; universities for subject content, resources and organisation; and colleges for personal support and staff-student communications.

The highest proportion of students who felt that they had made the right choice of course were in polytechnics. University students were the least positive.

10.10 Student Confidence

University students are consistently more confident than their peers; college students the least confident. University undergraduates are more bullish about passing their course, gaining good grades and obtaining suitable employment.

Far fewer university students intend to follow a career related to their study (60%) than do college and polytechnic students (80%). The latter are more likely to be studying on vocational, career-related courses.

10.11 Accommodation

The majority of university freshers start student life in halls of residence. To a lesser extent the same is true for the college undergraduate. In contrast, the great majority of polytechnic students have to find private sector accommodation. When we focus on those students in the private sector, it is the college fresher who had most difficulty in finding suitable accommodation. This is likely to be a result of the more rural/suburban nature of colleges: these places tend to lack the type of properties usually associated with student housing.

10.12   Finances

Over 50% of all students were in the red at the end of their first year. Slightly fewer university undergraduates were in debt than were polytechnic or college students. More polytechnic and college students suffer from getting neither a full grant nor full parental contributions; although more university students rely on parental support, a greater proportion do get it.

Of those with an overdraft, it is polytechnic students who, on average, have the greatest debt (£292) and the university student who has the smallest debt (£259).

Polytechnic and college freshers are much more likely to work during term-time than are university first-years (28%, 30% and 12% respectively).

10.13   Social Life

The great majority of university first-years join at least one social/sports club (87%). This is much less prevalent in the other two sectors.

When it came to identifying the most common problems that students suffer from, polytechnic respondents placed finance top, followed by housing; college students went for finance, followed by lack of confidence; university students also put finance top (although less strongly), with examination anxiety in second place.

Chapter 11   Conclusions and Recommendations

11.1   General

The research described in this book is rooted in personal experience and therefore many results relate to individual expectations. Whether these expectations are realistic will be judged by others, particularly those supplying careers advice and developing curricula in schools and colleges and those supplying the whole range of experience in higher education. It would be, at best, unwise and, at worst, arrogant to assume that the consumers' views are wrong simply because they do not accord with the perceptions of the providers.

There are of course certain absolute measures revealed by the survey, notably the indebtedness experienced by students which is likely to be exacerbated by legislation introduced after the survey had been completed which withdrew various social security benefits from students. Whether it is right or not that the students should receive social security is not the issue; what emerges from the research is the poverty under which students are having to think constructively, be stimulated intellectually and produce cogent output. It is clearly time to act now to pay students a decent (the minimum national?) wage if we are to avoid a situation in which our doctors, lawyers, engineers, bankers and so on claim that they are deficient in certain areas of their work simply because, when they were qualifying, they were unable to concentrate on parts of their course owing to a lack of food or heat! That is of course a somewhat facetious presentation but the point is made. No successful employer would expect his or her workforce to function effectively under the sort of conditions imposed on students.

The questions asked during the survey were detailed and they produced detailed answers. There are therefore all manner of specialist conclusions that can and will be reached which cannot easily be enumerated in a single concluding chapter. We both hope and assume that a wide variety of initiatives will be generated by our findings.

There are nevertheless two highly significant underlying problems which must be addressed by the correct solutions.

11.2   The Preparation for Higher Education Within School

We believe that this survey goes some way to explaining many of the findings in *Young People's Knowledge of Higher Education* (1) which revealed a depressing lack of knowledge about higher education (and confidence) in young people. This is particularly highlighted by the apparent lack of guidance at 16 + on A-level subject choice in so far as it related to potential options within higher education. We infer that there is even less guidance given to young people below that age, e.g. on GCSE subject choice, which is probably the time when inbuilt prejudice shown by many about, and indeed against, higher education could be addressed.

We would therefore like to see developed in our schools a client centred system of careers, education and pastoral advice in which guidance counsellors stay with individual pupils from say 11 or 14 + and help them steadily through their choices, both educational and careers, as they reach the various decision making times of their school lives. This contrasts strongly with the present practice of having specialists in school for higher education entrance (sometimes even broken down into Oxbridge or university entrance) for 18 + careers specialists, for 16 + leavers and so on. The responsibilities of these staff are by definition relatively strictly delineated and such staff deal with new cohorts of pupils as they reach their sphere of influence. There is therefore a tendency not to have a continuum of advice and this works to the disadvantage of pupils. We have noted that respondents to the survey were heavily dependent for advice about higher education on class and subject teachers, both categories of staff being likely to be in more regular and personal contact than is allowed for under current careers advice arrangements. This seems to contextualise the need for a continuous, client centred approach to careers and educational advice. Our proposal for revised counselling arrangements almost certainly implies a need for extra resources, for better training of guidance counsellors and probably for more of them. If the Government wishes to see appropriate use of higher education made by the third of all school-leavers which it hopes to see enter higher education by the year 2000, it would be false economy not to provide these resources.

At this stage we make no apology for returning to the debate about whether A-levels provide an adequate preparation for higher education. It has to be remembered that A-levels are much more than higher education entrance qualifications; they indicate also to the world of work how well students have performed at school. Yet the concerns expressed by some of the students in this survey, that A-levels are too narrow and depend far too little on students working in groups, would surely be echoed by employers who are looking in particular for employees with communications skills. We believe that A-level courses must be provided that reflect all the educational experience up to 16+ and educational and work experiences post 18+ i.e. ones of group-based work in which interpersonal relationships and communications skills are essential. Clearly, our survey suggests that BTEC courses and teaching methods have hit the right balance. Why can this not be achieved for A-levels?

One of the Government's most proudly boasted achievements in education has been the introduction of GCSEs with their new methods of teaching, learning and assessment. The government, rightly in our view, points to the GCSE as a significant factor in the increased participation in post 16 education. The Government will therefore get it all wrong if it proceeds to reduce the level of coursework in GCSE assessment, since it will precisely be undermining one of the basic reasons for the success of GCSE. It will doubtless still further reduce the effectiveness of A-level as a preparation for the collaborative working methods now increasingly required for higher education and employment.

Before turning to the second underlying concern realised by our research we return to an issue previously highlighted by *Young People's Knowledge of Higher Education* (1). We note that the reputation of the city or town in which the higher education institution is situated is the second most important factor in determining choice of institution (**Table 22**). This serves to underline the research (**1 and 5**) that shows that it is a marketing imperative that a higher education institution should be named after a large or well-known city or town; after all if the place is not well-known it is unlikely to have a reputation to be taken into account when choosing university, polytechnic or college option.

11.3   The Experience Within Higher Education

Within higher education some clear issues emerge that need not be developed here.

One theme does recur however: staff in higher education apparently receive little training, certainly on a compulsory basis, on what is expected of them. This is not to decry staff development schemes that exist in universities, polytechnics and colleges or the work carried out by the training units of the Committee of Vice-Chancellors and Principals or the Committee of Directors of Polytechnics. It is surely odd that whereas there is a very strictly regulated system of training teachers for work in schools in order that the best can be drawn from pupils, there is no requirement for staff in higher education to undergo any such training. It is surely not sufficient to expect to lay facts or opinions before students in a take or leave it fashion. Academic staff must be trained in techniques which will facilitate learning by students. We are all familiar with the expression "to read for a degree" but students must be inculcated with the means to be able to do just that. And it should go further. Staff in higher education should be instilled with techniques in counselling, personal and social education, motivation and other skills to enable them to develop the talents of both young and mature students. The notion that it is sufficient, indeed necessary, to have a researcher working at the cutting edge of his or her subject to lecture to or at students is quite clearly outmoded. First, an academic wishing to teach students need only embrace scholarship by reading about developments in the relevant subject or attending conferences and seminars. Research experience is unnecessary. Second, as basic governmental research funding is diminished over the next few years, far fewer academics will have research opportunities and it will behove them to develop the appropriate teaching skills.

But teaching is not the right word here. What is needed, rather more, are management skills. It is not a question of spoon feeding classes but of trying to get the best out of all the members of the 'class' or the 'work force' both as individuals and as a group. However such skills must be developed and whatever they are called, it is clear that there is no systematic or compulsory process of achieving them. But there should be. A concentration on the needs of the clients, the students, for whom higher education exists, would surely reduce the failings and frustrations suggested by this survey. Management skills for academic staff are imperative and they should be taught on a compulsory basis.

Finally, it should be emphasised that we have surveyed those in their second year of higher education, i.e. those who made the transition from school to higher education and then jumped the first major hurdle of getting beyond the first year. There will be those who just (only just?) crossed the Rubicon from school to university, polytechnic or college and then who thought that they had really reached the goal of higher education but who never got to second base. We believe that they should now be the subject of a comprehensive research programme.

REFERENCES

(1) *Young People's Knowledge of Higher Education* by Keen and Higgins. Published by Heist and PCAS 1990. ISBN 0 9512803 2 5. Available from Heist priced £9.95.

(2) Various surveys of students conducted by individual institutions have shown location to be of prime importance to candidates. Several (unpublished) Heist surveys have also highlighted the importance of place in the higher education marketing mix. Until recently most institutions believed that in terms of location they had been "dealt their hand" and therefore could do little to change the locational nature of their service. The recent "explosion" of franchising, the creation of associate colleges and the development of new facilities, such as those at Milton Keynes (Leicester Polytechnic) and the joint college of Teesside Polytechnic and Durham University at Stockton, show that there is more than one way to play the "locational hand".

(3) *A Two-Way Success*, a video training package on interview technique. Published by Trotman and Co Ltd 1991. Available from Trotman and Co Ltd, 12 Hill Rise, Richmond, Surrey TW10 6UA, price £26 including VAT and postage and packing.

(4) *Surviving the First-Year*—the experience of new teaching staff in higher education. SCED Publications, Learning Methods Unit, Birmingham Polytechnic, Perry Barr, Birmingham B42 2SU. Price £5.

(5) *Adults' Knowledge of Higher Education* by Keen and Higgins. Published by Heist and PCAS 1992. Available from Heist priced £11.95.

Appendix 1   The Questionnaire

Section 1. General Questions

1. Are you:

   1 Male
   2 female

2. What was your age at the time of starting your present course?

   _____ years

3. At the time of applying for a place on your current course, were you attending a:

   1 Comprehensive school
   2 FE or technical college
   3 Independent school
   4 Sixth-form college
   5 Grammar school
   6 Other (full-time education)
   7 In full-time employment
   8 None of the above

4. In which subject area are you studying?

   (If you are studying on a modular or joint honours course, indicate the subject area which accounts for the largest share of your study.)

   1 Engineering and Technology
   2 Built Environment
   3 Science and Maths
   4 IT and Computing
   5 Business/Management/Law
   6 Health and Social Services
   7 Humanities and Social Sciences
   8 Art and Design/Drama and Music
   9 Education and Teacher Training
   0 Medicine/Dentistry

   If you are uncertain of the category please write your course subject here:

   _____

5. What is the approximate distance from your current place of study to your parental home?

   1 0-19 miles
   2 20-39
   3 40-59
   4 60-79
   5 80-99
   6 100-119
   7 120-139
   8 140-159
   9 160 and above

6. On what type of course are you studying?

   1 Honours degree
   2 Degree
   3 DipHE
   4 HND
   5 Other

7. How many A-level points did you achieve before entering higher education? (AS-levels count for half value—e.g. grade A = 5 points)

   $E = 2\ D = 4\ C = 6\ B = 8\ A = 10$

   enter total here _____

   Please tick if you have other equivalent qualifications (e.g. HNCs, etc.)

   _____

8. What is the name of your institution? (i.e. the college at which you spent your first-year.)

   _____

9. At the time of applying to your present course, was your main place of residence located in a:

   1 Rural area/village
   2 Small town (10-50,000)
   3 Major town (51-200,000)
   4 City (201,000+)

Section 2. Initial choices

1. By what age had you firmly decided to aim for a place in higher education? (please circle one number)

   Aged   10   11   12   13   14   15

         16   17   18   19   20+

2. By what age had you firmly decided that your current subject was the one that you wished to study in higher education? (please circle one number)

   Aged   10   11   12   13   14   15

         16   17   18   19   20+

3. (a) Do you have a close friend or immediate relative who has a degree (or similar qualification), or who is employed in, a field related to your current studies?

   1 Yes
   2 No

   If No please go to Q4.

3. (b) If yes to (a), did you discuss your career/educational plans with them?

   1 Yes—in depth
   2 Yes—but not in depth
   3 No
   4 Can't remember

3. (c) If yes to (b), did they suggest specific institutions to which you should apply?

   1 Yes
   2 No
   3 Can't remember

4. Whilst in the sixth-form, did you seriously consider some form of employment as an alternative to higher education—i.e. apply for a job, write away for job details etc?

   1 Yes
   2 No
   3 Can't remember

5. Have either of your parents (or guardians) got a degree or an equivalent qualification?

   1 Yes
   2 No

6. If yes to Q5, please place an M(mother) and/or F(father) next to the appropriate description to indicate the type of institution they attended.

   _____ Teacher Training College
   _____ Art College
   _____ University
   _____ Open University
   _____ Polytechnic
   _____ Other type of HE college
   _____ Don't Know

7. (a) Before applying to higher education, did you have an interview with one or more of the following to discuss your future plans? (tick more than one if required).

   1 A careers adviser (normally based in a careers office or at your local council).
   2 A teacher specialising in careers/education counselling.
   3 The Head-Teacher/Principal
   4 Form teacher/house master
   5 A relevant subject teacher
   6 None of the above

   If you have ticked 6—None of the above, please move directly to Q9

126

7. (b) In light of your experiences, how would you rate the overall quality of the advice that you received from the adviser indicated in Q7(a)? (Please tick one)

Excellent Poor Good Bad Fair

8. Did your careers teacher or the careers adviser:

   (a) Recommend a specific institution of higher education to you, or suggest you apply there?
   1 Yes
   2 No

   (b) Recommend that you should apply to a certain type of institution as your first choice?
   1 Yes
   2 No

   (c) If yes to (b), did he or she recommend: (Please tick more than one if required)
   1 Polytechnics
   2 Colleges of HE
   3 Universities
   4 Specialist Colleges

9. After you had decided which subject you wished to study in higher education, what criteria did you use to short-list those institutions to which you would apply. Please list the three most important criteria in order of their importance to you.

   1................................
   2................................
   3................................

10. Was your present college the one that you most wanted to attend?
   1 Yes
   2 No
   3 Can't remember

Section 3—the admissions process

1. Did you attend an individual interview, or an open day, for your current course?

   1 Interview
   2 Open day
   3 Neither

   If you answered Neither to Q1 please go to Section 4.

2. Which words best describe the nature and atmosphere at that interview/open day?

   (Please tick as appropriate)

   1 Casual
   2 Formal
   3 Inspiring
   4 Dull
   5 Rigorous
   6 Easy

3. Did your interview visit or open day include any of the following: (Please tick those which were included)

   1 Contact with other applicants
   2 Contact with current students
   3 A tour of the college/dept
   4 A chance to talk to staff
   5 A video or AV presentation
   6 A chance to see "live" classes
   7 Time to tour the town/city
   8 Visit to the Student Union

4. On a scale of 1 to 10 how would you rate the induction or familiarisation procedures for new students starting your course? (1 = very bad, 10 = excellent)

   score _____

127

Section 4—Opinions of the College

1. Would you recommend your college to someone who was considering applying for higher education?

   1 Yes—definitely
   2 Yes—with some reservations
   3 Uncertain
   4 No
   5 Definitely not

2. (a) In your opinion what, in general, is the worst thing about your college? (please give one short answer)

   _____

   (b) In your opinion, what, in general, is the best thing about your college? (please give one short answer)

   _____

3. Would you recommend your course to someone who was considering studying in your subject area?

   1 Yes—definitely
   2 Yes—with some reservations
   3 Uncertain
   4 No
   5 Definitely not

4. How satisfied/dissatisfied are you with the following aspects of your institution? (rating 1 to 10, with 1 = very bad, 10 = excellent)

   _____ The Student Union
   _____ Sporting Facilities
   _____ Bars/Catering
   _____ Entertainment
   _____ Social Facilities/Clubs
   _____ Library/Learning Resources
   _____ Private Study Facilities
   _____ Computer/IT Support

5. Thus far, how would you rate the following aspects of your course on a scale of 1—10 (1 = very bad, 10 = excellent)

   _____ Organisation/Efficiency

   _____ Quality of the lecturing

   _____ Resources and equipment

   _____ Subject content

   _____ Personal support

   _____ Communication with staff

   _____ Student participation in course development

   _____ Overall learning experience

Section 5. Miscellaneous opinions

1. Having completed one year in higher education, do you think that you have made the right choice of course?

   1 Yes
   2 Uncertain
   3 No

2. Is the volume of work related to your course:

   1 More than you had anticipated
   2 Less than you had anticipated
   3 As you had anticipated?

3. On a scale of 1 to 10, how confident are you of passing your course? (1 = not at all confident, 10 = very confident)

   _____

4. For honours degree students only.

   Which classification do you expect to achieve at the end of your course?

   1 First
   2 Upper second
   3 Lower second
   4 Third
   5 Pass
   6 Fail

5. Do you intend to follow a career which is closely related to your course/subjects of study?

   1 Yes—definitely
   2 Probably
   3 Uncertain
   4 Unlikely
   5 No

6. On a scale of 1 to 10, how do you rate your chances of obtaining suitable employment within three months of graduation? (1 = no chance, 10 = certain)

   _____

Section 6. Aspects of college life

1. In what type of accommodation did you start your first year at college?

   1 Halls of residence
   2 Rented bed-sit
   3 Rented flat/house
   4 Parental/guardian home
   5 Room in lodgings
   6 Hostel
   7 Other (specify)

   _____

2. On a scale of 1—10, how easy/difficult was it to find suitable accommodation at the beginning of your first year? (10 = very easy, 1 = very difficult)

   _____

3. At the start of your first year, approximately how many miles did you have to travel from your accommodation to your usual place of study?

   _____ miles

4. In the first-year, did you have a job of some type during term-time?

   1 Yes—for most/all of the year
   2 Yes—intermittently
   3 No

5. If yes to Q4, on average, how many hours a week (7 days) did you work?

   _____ hours

6. If yes to Q5, what was the nature of the job? (If you had several jobs, give the main one) e.g. barman, dispatch rider etc.

   _____

7. During the first year, did you receive a full LEA grant ?

   1 Yes
   2 No

8. If No to Q7, did your parents/ guardians make up the grant in full through parental contributions?

   1 Yes
   2 No

9. Other than a grant and/or parental contributions, did you have any of the following sources of income during your first year? (tick more than one as necessary).

   1 Social security benefits etc.
   2 Wages (term-time work)
   3 Investment income
   4 Sponsorship
   5 Wages (holiday work)
   6 Other

10.At the end of the first year, were you in the red? (Please tick the appropriate number).

0 No—I was in the black
1 <£50 overdrawn (OD)
2 £51 to £100 OD
3 £101 to £150 OD
4 £151 to £200 OD
5 £201 to £250 OD
6 £251 to £500 OD
7 >£500 overdrawn

11.During your first year, were you a member of any student club or society based at your college?

1 Yes
2 No

12.During your first year, how regularly did you return home to visit relatives/parents/friends during term-time?

1 Once a week
2 Once a fortnight
3 Once a month (four weeks)
4 Once a term
5 Once a year
6 Never

13.Would you say that "making friends" at college in your first year was:

1 More difficult than you expected
2 Less difficult than you expected
3 As you had expected

14.Which of the following would you rate as the most common problems encountered by students during their first year? (please tick three)

A Feeling Depressed
B Drugs
C Anxiety
D Sexual problem
E Conflict with parents
F Relationships
G Lack of confidence
H Career indecision
I Financial problems
J Examination anxiety
K Homesickness
L Loneliness
M Physical illness
N Housing problems
O Alcohol problems

Appendix 2

INSTITUTIONS PARTICIPATING IN THE QUESTIONNAIRE SURVEY

University	Polytechnics	Colleges of HE
Aston	Birmingham	Anglia *
Bath	Bournemouth	Bangor Normal
Bradford	Brighton	Bath
Bristol	Bristol	Bolton Institute
Brunel	Coventry	Bretton Hall
Buckingham	Hatfield	Buckinghamshire
Cambridge	Humberside	Bradford and Ilkley
City	Kingston	Charlotte Mason
Durham	Lancashire	Colchester
East Anglia	Leeds	Cheltenham and
Essex	Leicester	Gloucester
Exeter	Central London	Dartington
Heythrop College	East London	Derbyshire
Hull	North London	Ealing *
Keele	Manchester	Edge Hill
Kent	Newcastle	Nene
Lampeter	Nottingham	Gwent
Leeds	Oxford	Homerton
Liverpool	Polytechnic South West	King Alfred's
Loughborough	Sheffield	Liverpool Institute
Newcastle	Staffordshire	London College of
Oxford	Sunderland	Fashion
Reading	Teesside	London College of
Salford	Wales	Printing
School of Slavonic		Luton
Studies, London		North Cheshire
Sheffield		New College Durham
Southampton		North East Wales
Sussex		Institute
UC Cardiff		North Riding
UC Bangor		Ravensbourne
UC Swansea		Ripon and York St John
UMIST		Roehampton Institute
Warwick		Royal Northern College
Wye College, London		of Music
York		St Mark and St John
		S Martin's
		Thames Valley *
		Trinity And All Saints
		West Glamorgan
		Worcester
		West Sussex Institute

* Subsequently designated a polytechnic

131

Appendix 3

INSTITUTIONS HOSTING FOCUS GROUP INTERVIEWS

Universities
East Anglia
Exeter
Southampton
Salford
Leeds
Brunel
Warwick
Cardiff
Nottingham
Durham

Polytechnics
Anglia (Chelmsford)
Newcastle
South Bank
Wolverhampton
Humberside
Manchester
Bristol
Brighton
Wales
Leicester

Colleges of HE
Derbyshire
Worcester
North East Wales Institute
Edge Hill
North Riding
Trinity And All Saints
Dartington
Homerton
Ealing College *
Thames Valley *

* Subsequently merged and
  designated as The Polytechnic of
  West London.

Appendix 4

1 Please tell me which subject you are studying and what led you to choose to study that subject?

2 When you were all aged 16 or so, you had to make decisions about which A-levels to study. How did you make those choices?

3 Thinking back to your school days, when did you really make up your mind about which subject you wanted to study in higher education? Who did you take advice from? Did anyone, or anything, in particular, influence your choice of degree/diploma subject?

4 Why did you decide to stay on in higher education rather than get a job or have a year off? What do students get out of higher education? What makes it worthwhile?

5 Think back to the interviews that you had for places in higher education. In light of your experiences, what advice would you give prospective candidates about interviews?

6 Did this college send you any information between the period of confirming your place and the course actually starting? Prompt... e.g. accommodation advice, reading lists, where to report, detailed syllabus, etc. If you were in charge of admissions to your course, what information would you send to new students to help them prepare for the course and college life?

7 Do you think that sixth-form or FE college study is a good preparation for higher education or not? In what ways, if any, is higher education study different to school or FE college?

8 In the past seven days (including the weekend) how many hours have you spent studying? By study, I mean lectures, tutorials, etc., and private study. Is the volume of work more or less than you had expected?

9 What sort of problems do first-year students encounter? Have you experienced any personal or study problems ? Is it easy to make friends? Are there people to listen when students have problems?

10 What are the best aspects of being a student here at XYZ College? What, if anything, makes the College special? What are the worst aspects of the College?

11 Are you satisfied with your course? What would you do to improve it? Would you recommend it to an interested applicant?

12 The transition from school to higher education can be challenging. What advice would you give to prospective students? Do you think that school-leavers need better advice on some issues? What, if anything, worried you before you started here?

Information about Heist

Formed in 1987, Heist is a unique company which is concerned with marketing and public relations in higher and further education. Although financially independent, Heist is supported by PCAS, NATFHE, BTEC, CNAA and Leeds Polytechnic.

In addition to its research function, Heist also organises conferences and workshops, publishes books and magazines, concerned with educational marketing. A range of consultancy services are also provided to individual institutions, ranging from prospectus editing and publications management, to market research and communications audits. Heist also provides a central distribution service for higher education prospectuses to schools and other centres throughout the UK and Europe.

Publications available from Heist include:

Young People's Knowledge of Higher Education (1990) by Keen and Higgins. Published by Heist/PCAS at £9.95 including postage and packing.

The full report of a survey involving over 7,000 sixth-form pupils in 691 schools/colleges which assessed the knowledge and perceptions of higher education amongst "traditional" applicants.

The book will be of interest to careers advisers in schools, LEAs and colleges, and to those responsible for recruiting students in higher education including the editors of prospectuses and course leaflets.

"It is essential that we help our young people to make informed choices—and here is a valuable and readable book to identify the gaps that we need to fill. It would also come as a salutary reminder of gaps in our own knowledge." (Newscheck with Careers Service Bulletin)

Adults' Knowledge of Higher Education (1992) by Keen and Higgins. Published by Heist/PCAS at £11.95 including postage and packing.

The report of a survey of over 4,000 adults which measures their knowledge and perceptions of higher education. Four groups were tested: access students, mature applicants to PCAS and UCCA, the parents of "traditional" applicants to UCCA and PCAS, and family friends of traditional applicants (not in higher education) but over 30 years old.

This report will be essential reading for those in higher education who have responsibility for widening access and recruiting mature students. Careers advisers in LEA offices, and those in central education organisations and government agencies will find the results of great value when counselling clients and drafting policy.

Public Relations Management in Colleges, Polytechnics and Universities (1988) by Keen and Greenall. Published by Heist at £10.95 including postage and packing.

This book covers the broader issues of public relations strategy, explaining both the nature and potential of professional public relations practice in the higher and further education environment.

"This book should be purchased by everyone who has the slightest interest in the promotion of their institution, be it a further or higher education college...." (THES)

Visual and Corporate Identity (1989) Edited by Keen and Warner. Published by Heist at £9.95 including postage and packing.

A study of identity programmes in the college, polytechnic and university environments.

"Anyone interested in design and corporate identity will find this a most interesting collection of essays, covering every aspect of the subject.... This moderately priced book can be recommended to all in public relations." (International Public Relations Review)

Promotional Publications: A Guide for Editors (1992) by Zoë Whitby. Published by Heist at £14.95 including postage and packing.

A comprehensive companion for editors working in all educational organisations who have responsibility for publications such prospectuses, annual reports and course leaflets. The book covers project management, print, design and photography, distribution, sub-editing, sponsorship and advertising, publications research and much more.

Publications edited by Zoë Whitby have won awards for prospectuses, annual reports and course leaflets.

Promoting Education A termly magazine published by Heist. Annual subscription £20 including postage and packing.

The magazine for public relations and marketing officers in further and higher education. Regular columns cover events and exhibitions, new reports and books, media update, the work of relevant support groups and the latest research.

Contributors include in-house practitioners, consultants and education journalists working throughout the UK and overseas.

Heist, The Grange, Beckett Park Campus, Leeds LS6 3QS. Tel (0532) 833184.

About the Authors

D J Roberts BA, M.Soc.Sc, MIPR

David Roberts is the Company Manager of Heist. He was previously Head of Marketing and Information at Nottingham Polytechnic, after spending four years in a marketing position with Leicestershire County Council.

He has published a number of articles on education marketing issues and is co-author of a number of reports concerned with local economic development. David is Editor of *Promoting Education*, a magazine for public relations officers in further and higher education.

M A Higgins BA, FBIM

Tony Higgins is the Chief Executive of the Polytechnics Central Admissions System (PCAS) and, as its first employee, was instrumental in developing its approach to managing applications to higher education beyond simply the bureaucratic to ensuring that all potential applicants, their families and advisers are well prepared to make the best of their application.

A frequent contributor to books on access to higher education, he is joint author (with Clive Keen) of *Young People's Knowledge of Higher Education* and *Adults' Knowledge of Higher Education*.

Prior to joining PCAS, he was an administrator at Leicester and Loughborough Universities during which time he was elected Chairman of the Conference of University Administrators.

In his spare time he is Chairman of the Haymarket Theatre Leicester, Vice Chairman of the Gloucestershire Everyman Theatre and works on the Development Committee of the Cheltenham International Festivals of Music and Literature. He is also Chairman of Heist.

Rob Lloyd (Researcher) MA, DipEd

Rob Lloyd was born in 1939. He was educated at Marlborough and Exeter College Oxford where he read Botany, led an expedition to Ecuador and captained his college rugby team. He took a DipEd at Oxford with a term's teaching practice at Leeds Grammar School. He has been Head of Biology at Sherborne School for about 15 years and at Melbourne Grammar School for two. He is now teaching Biology and advising on higher education at Sherborne School.

Rob Lloyd is the author of two books: *Man and Ecosystem* (1980) and *Chromosomes and Genes* (1985).